THE BEST OF MY FUN

The Best of My Fun

Christopher Curtis

with illustrations by
John Tickner
Rodger McPhail
Peggy Alexander
Carolyn Alexander
and a few less artistic efforts by
the Author

SWAN·HILL
PRESS

Copyright © Christopher Curtis, 1991.

First published in the UK in 1991
by Swan Hill Press.

British Library Cataloguing in Publication Data
Curtis, Christopher
The best of my fun.
1. Field sports
I. Title
799

ISBN 1 85310 174 5

Printed in England by Livesey Ltd., Shrewsbury.

Swan Hill Press
An imprint of Airlife Publishing Ltd.
101 Longden Road, Shrewsbury SY3 9EB, England.

Contents

Acknowledgements

Much of the material in this book has been provided, quite unwittingly, by people whose plans for a day's sport have been demolished by some untoward incident, or by the erratic behaviour of their animals. I am indebted to them all, aware as I am that, although immensely funny in retrospect, the incidents described may have seemed anything but at the time they occurred.

My grateful acknowledgements also go to the splendid artists who share my sense of fun and whose works adorn these pages. When I ran out of prose and turned to verse, John Tickner was on hand to illustrate my first effort. Since then he has produced drawings for many more, always accompanied by a letter asking me to return them if I wanted any improvements made; I never have. Rodger McPhail is renowned worldwide for his sporting and wildlife artistry. His outstanding ability as a cartoonist is shown in his contributions. Illustrations by Peggy Alexander, a sculptress, and Carolyn Alexander, an equestrian and wildlife painter are also included. The fact that they are, respectively, my mother-in-law and my sister-in-law has nothing to do with their inclusion; the quality of their drawings speaks for itself. To all of them I say thank you.

Two editors, of *Shooting Times and Country Magazine* and of *Horse and Hound*, were brave enough to publish many of the items that appear in this book. I am very grateful to both of them for allowing these stories and verses to resurface here.

Introduction

Being of an idle disposition, I have endeavoured, with some degree of success, to spend a decent proportion of my life in a sedentary position. At an early age, I exchanged the (to me) over-energetic pastime of cricket for what I thought would be a much more gentle exercise in paddling quietly up and down the River Thames, interspersed with rifle shooting, the only sport one can enjoy lying down.

My easy-going ambitions were somewhat thwarted by my hugely athletic schoolfellows and a housemaster whose aim was to win every sporting trophy available. I thus found myself being propelled at ever increasing speeds over the river and, during the winter months, forced to run about on cold, wet playing fields for the honour of the house. At least I managed to avoid the rigours of the School Corps by joining the Air Section, the activities of which were far less demanding.

Thence it was a simple passage to University, where more rowing was available and the Air Squadron, which provided an entree to the Royal Air Force in which I was to spend the best part of twenty years sitting, once again, this time in a cockpit. To be paid a reasonable salary at the same time as enjoying the fun of flying fighter aircraft was an added bonus.

More recently, my flying suit has been exchanged for breeches and my sitting down fun (when I am not forcibly ejected) continues in the hunting field. 'The Best of my Fun' are five words taken from Whyte Melville, who freely admitted that he owed it to horse and hound. In my case I must admit to owing a great deal to sitting whenever and wherever possible. I have, of course, had a lot of fun in positions other than sedentary. The printable occasions on which this non-sedentary fun has occurred are also reflected in the following pages.

Christopher Curtis.

Hunting

TO BOOT AND TO SADDLE

Circumstances combined, over a period of some twenty years, to keep me well away from horses. First, the design of fighter aircraft is such as not to allow space for the carriage of all the accoutrements required for riding, let alone the transport of a horse. Then, at a time when I might have ventured back into the saddle, an orthopaedic surgeon found it necessary to remove a bit of my back and I deemed it inadvisable to impose any additional strain on that part of my anatomy.

My employment by the British Field Sports Society changed all that. For some reason everyone took it for granted that someone in my position must automatically be a devil of a chap to hounds and I found myself turning down an embarrassing number of invitations to be a participant in a day's sport. Eventually, an invitation from my Chairman to stay for the weekend and to hunt was one which I felt I could not refuse — largely, I admit, because I did not wish to be thought guilty of cowardice; this, to a practising (but so far undetected) coward is important.

The day of the hunt was bright and sunny but the thought of the approaching Meet and all that might ensue hung like a black cloud on my mental horizon. On arrival at the Meet my horse was ready and waiting — and what a horse it was! My host was a man who is — how shall I put it — generously built and the mount he had provided for me looked large enough quite easily to carry both of us. A mild attack of vertigo passed off soon after I was hoisted aboard and it was with some relief that I found myself still in the saddle when we moved off.

Twenty years away from horses had erased the philology of the horse world from my memory, and when my host's son remarked of my horse in a friendly way, "Watch out, he hangs on a bit," I was none the wiser. While still pondering on the meaning of this possibly vital piece of information, I suddenly underwent the sort of acceleration normally only experienced by the pilots of supersonic aircraft when they cut in the afterburners. I slid rapidly towards the end of the horse from which the tail hangs and was only saved from falling off altogether by the reins. Clambering back into a more dignified position I endeavoured to reduce the speed at which my horse and of necessity I, too, were travelling. It immediately became apparent what 'hangs on a bit' meant. Nothing on earth would slow the animal down. In the course of the next 20 minutes and only barely remaining within Wiltshire's boundaries, we covered an enormous amount of ground at a very considerable speed. While unable to reduce my horse's forward velocity in any way, I did discover that maximum pressure on one rein had a marginal effect on the direction he took and it was thus that I eventually managed to rejoin the hunt at a point where they had checked.

This check served only to allow my mount to retrieve his breath and, when hounds set off in pursuit of their fox once again, he was electrified into an instant gallop. It was then, to my utter dismay, I discovered we were in a field entirely surrounded by a six-strand barbed wire fence. Employing the technique I had earlier found to have some effect, I persuaded him to encircle the field. Having broken the standing start lap record for this particular meadow by a large margin we arrived at the only gate to find it still blocked by some 40 members of the field waiting to get through. Hardly hesitating, my valiant steed veered slightly to one side and made straight for the fence. I did my best but, realising some six yards short of the wire that there was no stopping him, I closed by eyes and gave him his head. In jumping the fence he rose to a considerable height but it was nevertheless a lot lower than the altitude which I attained. Fortunately I retained my forward velocity and the parabola I described terminated back in the saddle when we reached the other side of this horrifying fence. On we galloped until alongside me came an immaculately clad rider. "Tell me," he enquired politely, "Do you always jump wire in your country, sir?" But by now my face was fixed in a rigid grimace, caused equally by strain and terror and I was quite unable to answer.

My next experience in the hunting field took place in Yorkshire after I had received an assurance that my proposed mount had no propensity for jumping wire. This was a hunt of a very different character. It seemed that no sooner had we left the Meet than hounds were in full cry down a steep hillside, up another one and finally up onto the high ground where we galloped and jumped, galloped and jumped. On the basis that my horse knew more about jumping than I did — a reasonable assumption in the circumstances — I let him do what he thought best. This worked very well for a time but, before long, muscles that had become atrophied through years of non-use began to ache and my limbs grew more and more tired. Sooner or later something unpleasant was bound to happen. It turned out to be sooner. The fox we were pursuing suddenly decided to make a sharp turn to the left. He was followed by the hounds, the huntsman, the field and my horse, but not, unfortunately, by me. The moment my horse chose to execute the turn came just as he touched down on the other side of a fence and, following my usual procedure, I had not at this point returned to the saddle, I therefore continued on in a straight line. While airborne I became inverted and then gradually lost altitude until my head came in contact with the ground. I thus ploughed a neat head-shaped furrow in an otherwise level Yorkshire field and converted my once immaculate office bowler into a muddy homburg.

An illustrious pack, noted equally for the quality of the

sport it offered and for the standard of sartorial perfection of those who followed it, provided the venue for my next day in the saddle. My recently purchased hunting clothes, topped by the aforementioned and restored bowler hat, had by now taken on an air of quaint if battered respectability. The effect was slightly marred by the cut that had been made in the top of my boot to allow for a swollen leg — the result of an earlier mishap. Initially, the gap was small but gradually it enlarged, allowing a considerable amount of my wife's nylon stocking which I was wearing to become exposed to view. It says much for the restraint of those present that no one commented on the sudden appearance in their midst of a swollen, hairy, nylon-clad leg. Most of the hazards that day turned out to be walls. This was a sad circumstance for me as I had earlier been warned that my mount had a tendency to investigate the other side of walls before actually jumping them. This meant that I was subjected to a fierce deceleration just short of each wall which inevitably resulted in my being propelled forward to a position immediately behind the horse's ears. However, the sub-sequent jump had the effect of returning me to a more central position. A refusal at one stage (caused by my own apprehension rather than the horse's) interrupted the sequence and prevented the restoration of the status quo. My subsequent progress, balanced on what I now know are referred to as the withers, was less than dignified.

At least until now I had not made an utter fool of myself and had fallen off under reasonably honourable con-ditions, but Nemesis was at hand. The next Meet I attended was a lawn meet, a truly social gathering with dutch courage being handed round in the form of stirrup cups. Suddenly my horse lay down. To retain one's dignity with a foot trapped under a horse, bowler hat askew and a glass in one hand is, I now know, an impossibility. A ring of human and equine faces looked down upon me with expressions of amazement and sympathy. Remounted, I felt happier again after a bit of hunting and when I had successfully negotiated several obstacles of varying heights. Some time later, relaxed and trotting along the road to a new covert, we rounded a corner. By the roadside lay a lump of machinery covered with a sheet of cellophane and it was as I passed it that the covering, caught by a gust of wind, blew up in my horse's face. He shied, reared up and slipped, any one of which would have sufficed to remove me from the saddle. The combination of all three had the effect of shooting me through the air, culminating in a three-point landing on a very hard piece of tarmac.

Fortuitously, my ankle, hip and elbow had made contact with the forecourt of an inn and I found myself looking up into the startled face of a man quaffing a pint of beer. Thrusting the reins into his free hand, I made my way shakily in through the door marked 'Saloon'. When I rejoined the hunt some time later, I was asked by a kindly lady if I was all right, with the added comment, "I hope you had a pint of beer while you were there." I nodded and smiled happily back at her, remembering the three large brandies I had downed during my enforced absence from the chase and which had, partially, restored my nerve.

In spite of such a poor start, I persevered and now have my own horse. The intervals between falls are still depressingly short and increasing age and weight ensure that I gravitate earthwards with a great deal more force than did Newton's apple. I have, however, the greatest faith in the continued ability of the medical profession to keep me roadworthy — at least for a few more seasons.

A GOOD TENPENNYWORTH

It is not every day that one gets stabbed, comes under heavy machine-gun fire and has to beg a lift back from hunting in a passing lorry, so I think it is worth recording the facts. Lest I might be accused of garnishing the tale with untruthful spice, I should mention that there are a number of reliable witnesses to the whole affair.

Although the events of which I write occurred in late January, in order to put the whole affair in its proper perspective, it is first necessary to return to the middle of the previous summer and, in particular, to the day when the local branch of the Riding for the Disabled Association held their annual Fête. Now a fête, if not actually worse than death, certainly registers high on my list of least favourite forms of entertainment. Gina, however, enjoys them and duly represented the family on this occasion, returning thence with, among other purchases, the most beautiful pair of breeches. Lovat green in colour, with a delicate blue cross check, made of real quality cloth and apparently unworn they were. On this useful garment Gina had expended the princely sum of ten pence.

The reason for the knock-down price only became

obvious when I tried them on, to discover that, although they fitted perfectly, the breeches were constructed after the fashion of yesteryear with absolutely enormous 'wings'. My appearance in them caused such mirth that some minutes passed before the family recovered sufficiently to pass a unanimous vote against their ever being worn by me in public. They therefore lay unused in a drawer for some months before the coincidence of a bye-day and my other breeches not having recovered from a series of muddy days gave me the chance to don them.

Bearing in mind the earlier threat by one of our Joint Masters to send me home should I dare to appear in the breeches, I took care to mount out of sight and most of the offending cloth was hidden beneath the flaps of my jacket by the time I hove in sight. Not appreciating that we were to be entertained at the Meet, I had earlier downed a couple of quick ones, an action I was almost immediately to regret when approached by an aged retainer with a vast tumbler about one third full of neat whisky. Before I could accept it, however, he extracted from under his arm a bottle of the same stuff, the contents of which he sloshed into the glass until it was full up to the brim.

Even in spite of this gargantuan spiritual measure, all might have been well had not James, who had lulled me into a false sense of security by behaving impeccably until then, chosen the moment when hounds moved off to put in a quick one. This unscheduled movement coincided with my attempting to drain the glass, causing the contents to shoot to the back of my throat, thereby inducing a choking fit and a sharpish performance of the elephant trick. Endeavouring to cover this unedifying spectacle with a hand, I inadvertently disconnected my stock pin, the point of which penetrated my hand and released a gush of blood to join the whisky pouring out of my nose and the tears streaming from my eyes.

I had recovered enough by the time we climbed up to the first draw to admire the superb views of the dale in which we met, renowned alike for its picturesque land-scape and its cheese. Recovered enough, too, to notice that I was not the only beneficiary of our hostess's liberal hospitality, for there was an air of unrestrained jollity among the field. Perhaps it was this that decided the Field

Master to lead us on a warm-up canter alongside the covert. Should this seem in no way remarkable, I must explain that the wood is hung on steep hillside and topped by a cliff at the edge of which runs a track. The track is not only narrow, winding and slippery, but liberally dotted with trees, the over-hanging branches of which force the rider to duck frequently or risk being swept over the cliff. We were all warm by the time we reached the end and even warmer when, the draw being blank, we did an about turn and reversed the process.

Hounds were quickly away from the next covert and, after a short scamper, we pulled up beside a fir wood in which our quarry sought temporary refuge. Here I was sent to a vantage point from which I soon observed some caps aloft by the roadside and heard excited holloas. Deeming a fox to be afoot and having identified the bared heads as belonging to normally reliable fellows, I had added the odd "Whooi!" to the general din before discovering, to my horror, that Charles had been seen in and not leaving covert. Luckily, hounds disregarded me and left the wood by another exit in close pursuit, so my misdemeanour passed unnoticed — almost. Unusually for me I had surmounted a gate on the way, and, by the time I had renegotiated this object, I was well behind.

Delays caused by first one and then another Master becoming entangled in wire gave me the chance to make good the deficit and I was catching up nicely as our fox took us over a number of walled grass fields and set his mask for the moors. Whether he was colour-blind and failed to notice the red flags or preferred the risk of a chance bullet to the more obviously pressing danger behind him, I do not know. He kept straight on into the sound of heavy firing which became ominously loud as we too advanced on to the moor. Firing ceased ("Thank God, they're friendly!" I thought) at about the same time that a diminution in scent slowed our progress, thus giving the Range Officer a chance to take a hand in the proceedings. Although too far away to hear his words of greeting, it was obvious that we were not altogether welcome. While the terms of the treaty were being worked out and feeling the need (it was a chilly day) to dismount, I took advantage of a wall. That the wall was not high enough I did not realise until a number of extremely unfunny remarks about my breeches were made when I rejoined the field, by now beating a retreat under a white flag.

Out on the road, it was a minute or two before I noticed that James, instead of his customary clip-clop, clip-clop, was going phut-clop phut-clop. From this I was able correctly to deduce that his front shoes were embedded somewhere among the spent bullets. Once again I had to dismount to a chorus of ribald comments, acutely conscious that my slightly undersized ratcatcher jacket was doing little to conceal the voluminous olde worlde appearance of my nether garment. Gina took James, I took her whip and walked up to the main road for a lift back to the trailer with one of the car followers. Sadly I arrived in time to see the last of the cars, filled to overflowing with others on the same mission, disappearing down the road.

So there I was, looking like a First World War Cavalry Officer whose horse had been shot from under him (not so far from the truth as it happened) and waiting for a passing limber to take him back to the rear lines. The limber duly appeared in the shape of a huge lorry, which, to my surprise and with a hissing of airbrakes, pulled up in response to my hopefully extended thumb. Brave fellow that driver. Had it been me in his place, driving through the wintry gloom of a lonely moor and seeing a man wearing kinky boots, two whips in one hand, making odd gestures with the other and a hopeful smile on his face, I would not have stopped. I would have put my foot hard down and dialled 999 at the first opportunity.

My benefactor dropped me at the entrance to a quarry a few miles down the road, opposite which, amazingly, was yet another lorry driver willing to accept me as a passenger. This second Samaritan deposited me in the market square of Leyburn with still a mile and a half to go. Happily, my exposure to the gaze of an astonished general public was shortlived. I had barely reached the outskirts of town when I espied a hunt car follower who, taking pity, turned round and took me the rest of the way. I was back at the farmhouse rendezvous almost as quickly as those who had employed more orthodox means of transport.

One way and another it had been an entertaining day — what you might call a good tenpennyworth.

PAST MY PEAK?

There I was, on top of this rocky crag, for all the world like a chamois surveying his mountainous domain. Perhaps I have overdrawn the analogy a trifle, for in truth I was more like a damp chamois leather which, if you think about it, is only a chamois with all the stuffing knocked out of it. The reason for both my altitude and my exhaustion was my introduction to fell hunting, a pastime which combines sport and high speed mountaineering.

My guide for the occasion, a native of the area, treated the near vertical hillside with all the disdain of a London clubman breasting the slope of St James's Street on the way to his pre-luncheon dry martini. Not so his disciple. I lived at the time in a part of the country where a morning's work by any reasonably fit mole would qualify for a contour line on the map. To be transported suddenly into Himalayan-like terrain and be expected to scale the heights came as a bit of a shock to the nervous system. Still, if that New Zealand chap could reach the top of Everest without even the hope of finding a fox at the top, I was not going to be defeated.

Though I write when the sharper details of the nightmare climb are shrouded in the kindly mists of time, I can say in retrospect that the sense of achievement and the view of arrival at the top made it seem worthwhile. I can well understand the wild surmise with which stout Cortez surveyed the distant Pacific as he stood silent upon a peak in Darien. I doubt, however, if he suffered as much as stout Curtis reaching his peak in Cumberland. Had he done so he would not have stood silent but, like me, he would have been lying there blowing like a grampus. At first, the glorious confusion of the fells tumbling away into the distance seemed more like ocean rollers about to pound a shipwrecked mariner on the rocks but gradually I got my breath back and was able to appreciate my surroundings.

Not for long, though. A large sandy-coloured dog fox, the killer (so I was told later) of many a lamb, slipped through the rocks beneath us and set his mask for the valley below. He was shortly followed by hounds, the huntsman, the field and, perforce, by me. Immediately I found myself in even more trouble. My legs, reduced to a sort of rubbery substance by the climb, were scarcely capable of supporting my body, let alone maintaining it in a vertical position during the descent. My return to the valley was therefore even less dignified than the climb out but a great deal quicker. At one point in my precipitate descent I disturbed a crow. I have no doubt that the startled caw it emitted as it leapt out of the way meant "Look out, chaps! There's fourteen stone of potential carrion on the way down." I did survive, but only just. The rest of the day I spent at valley level, content to watch the pursuit through my glasses.

As soon as I had accepted an invitation for a second visit to the fell country, I set about thinking of ways in which to survive the rigours of what promised to be a very energetic week. Short of enlisting the services of a couple of Sherpas, it seemed obvious that the frontal attack method I had employed previously was doomed to failure. I resorted instead to a stratagem which, with hindsight, I can recommend to others who may be short of wind and flabby of leg.

It involved picking the brains of some local hunter as to the likely lie of a fox and the direction of the first draw. One must then avoid the Meet and head straight for a suitable height which commands a view of the area. It is then possible to take one's time about achieving the chosen summit with plenty of pauses to admire the view and regain one's breath. The only equipment I have found essential to this form of hunting is a stick of good strong wood and a flask of good strong whisky.

Granted a fox in approximately the right place, one of two things may happen. Either he runs straight up the side on which one is standing, or he goes the other way. In the first case one has the pleasure of watching the other hunters, those made of sterner stuff or, perhaps, less gifted with foresight, toiling up towards one. In the latter case a glorious view can be had of the hunt as it develops along the opposite ridge. Eventually the hunt disappears and again one is faced with two alternatives, to descend and attempt to make contact again or to descend to the nearest pub.

The undoubted scenic pleasures of the fells are, to my mind, enhanced by the nomenclature employed throughout the district. Names such as Troutbeck recall hunting days long gone. Then, appropriately situated just north of Wordsworth's Cottage, are such poetic names as Stybarrow Dodd, Striding Edge and Dollywaggon Pike. On one drive I stopped to look up the name of a hill I was passing to discover that it had the charming name of Darling Fell. Round the next corner was a sign saying Darling How. Their juxtaposition seemed like a snippet of conversation overheard at a debutantes' ball, perhaps a discussion about some young lady's descent from grace.

If stamina is a requirement for the follower of fell fox hounds, no less is it an essential when hunting is over for the day. For the southerner, reference to a Hunt Ball or Hunt Dinner may conjure up visions of starched shirts, elegant tail coats, haute cuisine dishes, high fashion dresses and high-spirited cavortings on the ballroom floor.

In the fells, such is the frequency with which such celebrations are held, elegance and spaciousness have been discarded in favour of more practical clothing for the three main events of the evening — eating, drinking and singing. Had my constitution been capable of withstanding such an onslaught, I could have accepted invitations to a party every night of my stay — and one or two lunchtime ones as well.

Until I visited this part of the world I had always thought various writers' descriptions of tables and sideboards 'groaning under the weight of food' as over-indulgence in the use of descriptive licence. No longer, not after attending a fell hunt dinner. Quite frankly, I would not have been surprised had the table at which I sat let out a scream of agony, such was the volume of edibles placed upon it. Veritable mountains of cream cakes, bread and butter, salads, jellies, gateaux and pastries rose high enough to prevent one seeing the person sitting opposite. Tier upon tier they rose like some pastrycook's vision of the fells themselves.

It was an astonishing sight, but no more so than the one which followed. Dinner was advertised as 7.30 for 8p.m. At 7.20 sharp the hungry hordes poured in and set about the tables like a demolition team working on double time. Well before the appointed hour for dinner the tables were bereft of all but a few crumbs. Only contented smiles and a few discreet burps were left as evidence of the achievement of this monster disappearing trick.

And then it was time for 'a bit of a sing'. The requirements are simple. Any room capable of holding about 50 people with a bar at one end will do. Then put about two hundred into it and start singing. There is no accompaniment and voice training is not a prerequisite. Most of the songs are in the form of long tales about huntsmen and hunting, interrupted only by rousing choruses and occasional noises from the direction of the bar. The latter are invariably followed by loud 'Shushes' and calls for order from the Master of Ceremonies. And so the evening goes on. The atmosphere thickens, a distinct smell of damp terrier pervades the room, much beer is drunk and not a little spilt and the singing continues until well into the morning.

Long before the end, exhausted from a day's hunting, eating and drinking, I had crept away to my bed upstairs. Even the final chorus of Peel's View Halloo (rendered as only it can be in the heart of John Peel's country), whatever it may have done to those in the cemetery or to foxes in their lairs, failed to disturb my subsequent slumbers.

PRIDE BEFORE A FALL

I am writing this at a time when a number of hunts, ours amongst them, have finished their seasons. Memories of all but the very best days were beginning to fade, jackets and boots had been put away for several months and horses were being roughed off.

The season had not, however, finished for me. Tuesdays and Thursdays, 11a.m. sharp it was for me and these appointments kept the memory of the past season sharp in mind — for they were with a physiotherapist. When my bi-weekly treatments failed to revive sporting memories, a pain in my shoulder, which became particularly acute at about two o'clock every morning, brought them quickly back into focus.

It was, for me, a somewhat unfortunate season, the one in question. It started off well enough with my being given a horse — always useful if you want to ride across country. My equipment was further added to with the donations of a beautiful silk topper by my father-in-law and a splendid old-fashioned black coat by a friend. I was also lucky enough to buy a perfectly fitting and completely unused pair of boots for a price little more than one has to pay for a pair of new shoes these days.

Thus accoutred I set off for the opening meet full of pride in my appearance and with every expectation of good things to come. Nor was I, at first, disappointed. My new horse, James Bond no less, did everything that could be expected of him — which is quite a lot when I am riding. My horsemanship being what it is, I expect my horse to know rather more about the job than I do. When we come to a fence, I rather leave him to decide how to tackle the business. James appeared to accept this and, if he stopped once or twice, he did it in such a way that we both remained on the same side of the fence and never seemed to take offence at being asked to try again.

There were even days when we, though I dare not say distinguished ourselves, at least did passing well and were not far from the front at the end of a good run, or two. Confidence grew with every day spent in the hunting field. Then it happened.

Foxes were hard to find that day and, when one finally came out of a wood we had just drawn, it went the wrong way. This meant that we had to retrace our steps down a waterlogged track at the side of a ploughed field. With a hundred horses cantering in a close line astern behind us, James put his foot in a hole, nosedived and put his rider upside down in two foot of watery mud. Before a hoof, whose I know not, caught me a glancing blow on the side of my head, I remember seeing my precious top-hat, hit squarely by another hoof, sailing through the air at a speed that would have done credit to an England centre forward.

My appearance, when finally I managed to extricate myself from the gooey mass in which I had been deposited, was not unlike a very badly over made-up black and white minstrel. My hat was brought back to me looking as though it had just been entered in a chocolate cake icing contest. As for poor old James, every facial orifice was entirely blocked with mud and he could neither smell, see nor hear.

It was fortunate, indeed, that there was a deserted farmhouse nearby with a huge watertrough beside it. James' and my faces were treated first and then on down until I finished up standing in the trough removing some of the deadweight from my boots. My hat was the last item to be immersed.

This incident, which was followed later in the day by James and I finding ourselves for the first time on opposite sides of a fence, unnerved us both a little and it was a week or two before, once again, we were crossing country with our previous sang froid. And thus it went until what should have been the penultimate hunt of the season but turned out to be the ultimate.

The occurrence which so abruptly ended my season had, like its predecessor, absolutely nothing to do with the normal hazards of the hunting field. Not for me the glory of a treble somersault at a double oxer, a crumpling crash at a big drop or even a dip in the open ditch. For me merely the ignominity of a fall in a farmyard.

For an account of what happened I have, of necessity, to rely on the evidence of others, my own recollection of the incident being limited to the sight of a mass of metal approaching me at high speed and a distant voice saying, "For God's sake don't move the old b . . ." Apparently all four of James' legs slipped as we rounded a corner at the gallop and I became the centre piece of a sandwich, the outside layers of which were formed by my horse and a large farm roller, a part of which inconsiderately buried itself in my right leg.

However, Samaritans were at hand. One took me back to where we had met, another removed my boot and a third took me to hospital. Meantime, my wife, finding herself joined by my empty horse, had been reassured by a number of optimistic liars that I was quite all right and couldn't understand why I was making such a fuss and a small boy was heard asking his father if Mr Curtis was *really* dead.

Have you ever had to go to a hospital on a Saturday? If not, I strongly advise against it. For a start, the casualty department was closed — casualties presumably not being expected to be casual enough to happen outside Monday to Friday working hours or at least to be British and bear it until Monday morning. The main building did at least have a doctor in it but he was up to his elbows, literally for all I know, in other people who had been inconsiderate

16

enough to become involved in weekend mishaps. I was stuck in a small windowless foyer about the size, appropriately enough, of a coffin and told I could not have a cup of tea "In case you have to be operated on". I forebore to mention that I had just drained a large flask of whisky and cherry brandy and consoled myself by obliterating a NO SMOKING sign with clouds of exhaled smoke from an endless stream of cigarettes while an equally endless stream of patched up people passed through.

Eventually it was my turn, I was stitched up but not X-rayed — "No X-rays at weekends, you know," and driven straight to a number of very large whiskies.

As it happened, nothing was broken, though I found myself in complete agreement with the enormous number of people who kept telling me that torn shoulder muscles were just as, if not more painful than a broken shoulder. Thus came my bi-weekly physiotherapal visits and the difficulty I had in using my right arm, even for such activities as typing. It was, therefore, with some relief and a certain amount of pain that, to the end of that particular hunting season, I put the final.

UNHAPPY NEW YEAR

The year ended on a bad note — or, rather, on a discord, for there was more than one bad note involved. Come to think of it, I cannot remember a worse New Year's Eve save, possibly, the one when I was Duty Officer in a far-flung outpost and an officer who had, as they say, of the drink taken, decided to celebrate in an unusual way. Swaying into the bar of the Officers' Mess, he laboriously drew a revolver from his belt and announced his intention of shooting the bottles off the back of the bar.

It was obvious from the first shot, which penetrated the ceiling, that his aim was somewhat impaired. Even Abdul the barman, whose grasp of the English language was limited to a few brand names, got the message and turned from dark mahogany to a shade of greenish white, I just had time to notice this before assuming a prone position on the floor together with a shower of plaster and the padre to whom I had been talking. The next five rounds also failed to find a target and, deeming it safe to raise my head, I discovered that the would-be sharpshooter had left. Heading the posse which tracked him to his room, I saw the New Year in trying to persuade him to come out quietly, but my earnest pleadings were continually interrupted by renewed bursts of firing from within, sounds of splintering woodwork, the occasional tinkle of glass and the angry whine of ricocheting bullets.

Eventually his voice announced that he was going to shoot himself, there was a bang and then silence. Fearing a trap, we allowed a decent interval before rushing the door. We need not have worried. Maintaining his inaccuracy to the end, he had missed himself and fallen sound sleep.

Back now to the year's ending of which I write. It was, as I have indicated, a series of incidents, rather than a particular one, which combined to bring the year to an unsatisfactory close. During the days succeeding Christmas, frost, fog and snow had alternated with dismal frequency and made it certain that there was no possibility of hunting on New Year's Eve. It was, therefore, with some confidence that I made a number of appointments for the last day of the year. And then it thawed.

By morning, most (though not all, as I was to discover to my cost later) of the ice had gone, the sun shone from a cloudless sky and the prospects for hunting looked good. Donning nether garments suitable for hunting, I shook off the sloth engendered by several days of over-indulgence and set off for my first appointment. Arriving sharp at the agreed time of 8.30, I could see through the window the 100 picture frames I had ordered, but the shop was closed and otherwise empty. After a search of the bottom of the car, my step-daughter unearthed the required coin of the realm, thus enabling me to make a telephone call and establish the likely whereabouts of the chap who should have been there to meet me.

Being given the wrong address delayed things a bit, long enough in fact to be told, on arriving at the correct one, "You've just missed him." Back to the shop, from which, held up at a crossing some 50 yards distant, I was able to observe my quarry pull out in a van and disappear into a stream of traffic. There seemed little doubt that it was not going to be my day. Nor was it.

My next visit was to a house, the surrounds of which had been systematically drilled by the gas men throughout the night. This probably accounted for the less than enthusiastic welcome I received from its inhabitants at 9a.m., but at least it was better than my last call, where, once again, I drew a blank.

The state of dudgeon I had by now achieved could fairly be described as extremely elevated, but its altitude was reduced somewhat by my wife's suggestion that she should take horse and trailer to the meet, leaving me to follow on. With this excellent suggestion I concurred, for it gave me time to fill my flask *and* get to the Meet on time.

When we met up again, I paid scant attention to Gina's remark that she had had a "little contretemps" on the way to pick up James. I should have known better; in her language, "a near miss" means a respray, "a slight scrape" means one side of the car is missing and "a bit of a bump" is a complete write off. Even a Volvo will not withstand a head-on collision with a horsebox and, in spite of her assurance that "we were hardly moving", that car was never the same again.

The Meet was in the town square and liberal stirrup cups were dispensed by wenches in period costume. James did his usual party trick of attempting to sweep aside a drink laden tray and followed this with a determined grab at some passing sausage rolls. Apart from this the Meet passed without incident and things began to look up when, soon after setting out, a fox left cover and we managed to negotiate one or two jumps without mishap.

But scent, like my luck, was lacking that day and the hunt petered out, to be followed by a series of blank draws. Proceedings were temporarily enlivened by some fairly stiff artificial jumps in the middle of a wood and there was then a long hack down a road to the next draw, before which we were again faced with some artificial jumps. There had been plenty of time to sample the contents of my flask by now and this had engendered a thoroughly misplaced confidence, causing me to roar into the first fence handily placed behind the Field Master and just in front of a large number of hard riders. James chose this moment to put in his by now almost traditional stop of the day.

Not for the first time I was struck by similarities between my experiences as a pilot and in the hunting field. Once, having just landed on an aircraft carrier and while still taxi-ing forward, the deck crew suddenly vanished sideways into the safety nets and it became apparent that the pilot of the following aircraft had committed an error of judgment and was about to land on top of me. On that occasion, as this, it only required a quick glance over my shoulder to establish the seriousness of my position. Happily surviving both incidents, I learnt a number of things.

First, that it is possible to undo all one's straps and evacuate a cockpit in under one second. On this later occasion I discovered that there is, among the local hunting fraternity, considerable doubt as to the authenticity of my family tree and that some of them even thought I should do things which I would have thought were anatomically impossible.

This advice caused me to assume a more modest position in the field and I was pleased to find that James' jumping prowess was in no way impaired by the unfortunate episode when hounds fairly screamed away after a fox in the late afternoon. We were soon jumping with gay abandon, that is until, in mid-air, I noticed that the landing side of the jump we were above consisted of an ice-covered track. This fact escaped James' notice and, in spite of my best efforts to discourage him, he endeavoured to turn sharp right on touch down. We thus found ourselves facing in a southerly direction while still travelling eastwards at undiminished speed. Not for long, though. When James' feet met the plough, he tipped over, leaving me to continue on an easterly and, inevitably, downward course.

James recovered quickly and, by the time I had picked myself and one of my leathers out of the plough, he was fast disappearing, still jumping immaculately, into the distance. It was what you might term an inhorspicious ending to the year's hunting. Half a mile further on I was reunited with James, thanks to a lift from a car follower, only to find that the other leather was missing. This, by dint of retracing James' hoofprints, I was able to retrieve, but by then the hunt was over.

On returning home I found that the picture frames had been delivered. There were only sixty-four, of which half were the wrong size.

THE IMAGE OF WAR

It was William Somerville who, way back in the 18th century, described hunting as "the sport of Kings, Image of War, without its guilt" and Robert Surtees who, much later and through the mouth of John Jorrocks, added the equally immortal "and only five and twenty per cent of its danger."

When you come to think of it, there are a number of similarities in the make-up of a hunt and an army. The Commander-in-Chief is, of course, the Master. He controls overall strategy while his Corps Commander, the huntsman, directs tactics in the field, relying heavily, as does any tactical commander, on his intelligence services in the shape of earth-stoppers, farmers, gamekeepers and the like.

The thrusters, fanning out in front, represent the light cavalry, with the field, the heavy brigade, following on behind. They, in turn, are followed by the support groups of stoppers and gate shutters and the pioneer corps in the shape of the fence menders. Infantry, motorised and foot, are represented by the foot followers. Only the stretcher bearers are missing — and there *are* times I can remember when their services would have been appreciated.

My own experience of ground warfare is meagre, limited in fact to a few exercises with the school corps. Indeed, the only time I can remember having discharged a service rifle at other than a stationary target was during an exercise in Windsor Great Park when, unsuccessfully as it happened, I endeavoured to cause the demise of a royal pheasant by means of a pencil propelled up the barrel by a blank cartridge. Shortly after that I transferred to the air branch of the corps.

You might think that to draw comparisons between the art of flying and riding would be stretching the elasticity of one's similes to breaking point. Not so. Having spent a fair number of years manoeuvring single seat fighters about the sky and, more recently, a few seasons navigating across country on horseback, I have found many similarities in the two occupations. Careful handling and the occasional quick decision are needed in both cases, while take-offs and landings need care and judgment whether one is riding in a saddle or a cockpit.

There are, when it comes to low level flying and cross-country riding, some obvious differences — the higher speed of the former, for instance, leading to a likely fatal outcome in the event of contact with a stationary object. And the avoidance of the attention of enemy ground gunners, one of the objects of low flying, can hardly be compared with the, fortunately, remote possibility of meeting an armed and angry landowner during a day's hunting — though you never know. The sheer exhilaration of crossing a good line of country at speed is, however, common to both, as is the need for continual quickness of thought and reaction, if disaster is to be avoided. So, too, is the delicious retrospective savouring of the more thrilling moments of the flight or hunt, in debriefing room or bath as the case may be.

In regard to the safety of the pilot, there is no end to the provision of ingenious devices, such as safety straps, parachutes and ejector seats, facilities which, to my mind, would be welcomed by many an equestrian. The forces of gravity and inertia encountered in flying are admittedly greater than when riding; I have never been advised by the Field Master, as I was by the Fight Deck Officer, to remove my false teeth prior to take off, for example. Nevertheless, they have frequently been strong enough to bring about my displacement from the saddle.

Take the time when, due to an error of judgment, I found myself entwined in the barrier erected on the deck of an aircraft carrier. Since the purpose of the barrier is to prevent one charging into the aircraft parked for'ard, the cessation of forward movement is fairly abrupt and the need for straps fairly obvious. The desirability of straps while riding across country was admirably illustrated by a remarkable photograph of myself taken by Roy Parker.

It shows my horse above a jump and me about 3'6" above the saddle. This incident occurred at the end of a long, cold and wet day's mounted stewarding and, in part at least, was caused by the generosity of friends and the close proximity of a bar to my place of duty. That I returned to the saddle without incurring a double injury must be classified as a major miracle.

It is when we come to Mr Jorrocks' assessment of the danger ratio in warfare and hunting that I find myself in disagreement, limited though my experience in both may be. Various torn ligaments, strained muscles, the odd broken bone and innumerable cuts and bruises bear ample witness to the perils of the hunting field, whereas, during nearly 20 years of flying, I suffered not a scratch. Indeed, on only one occasion while engaged on operational flying can I remember having even come close to disaster. This happened when, during a low level attack on some intransigent Arabs, I discharged a missile which rebounded with such force that I nearly achieved the unenviable distinction of scoring an own goal.

I am full of admiration for those bold ladies and gentlemen prepared to take their own line across country. At the same time, being fully aware of my own limitations in nerve and ability, I have no desire to emulate them, being quite content to let others savour the thrills of jumping into the unknown.

When a straightnecked fox sets his mask towards a useful looking piece of country, hounds in close pursuit and the thrusters not far behind them, I find myself, once again, comparing this life with a former one. Was it Whyte

Melville or Surtees who said of hunting: "Happy is he who sets out to enjoy himself and not to astonish others"? Whoever it was, he must have had the same thought in mind as the more modern anonymous inventor of the oft-repeated airman's creed: "There are *old* pilots and there are *bold* pilots, but there are no old bold pilots."

Comforting myself with these two maxims, I settle happily into a position somewhere in mid-field. Who knows? I might yet survive a few more seasons.

The 20th Century Fox

Illustrated by John Tickner

They call me Charles James and a few other names,
Such as Reynard and Charlie the Fox.
I'm a glutton for hens and for turkeys in pens
And a worry to men who tend flocks.

People cut quite a dash and they pay out good cash
When it's me that they're huntin' y'know.
I'm a hell of a fellow, just hear how they bellow,
"Forrard on!" — "Gone away!" — "Tally ho!"

Hounds and horses all rush in pursuit of my brush
When, with hats raised, they shout, "Gone away!"
Then I lead hounds a dance and they haven't a chance,
For I know they'll not catch me today.

When the day's sport is done and they've all had their fun,
Do you know what I'm going to do?
First, I'll dine on a pheasant and my dreams will be pleasant,
For hunting is **my** *pleasure, too.*

Tally Ho Back!

There are verses galore about great hunts of yore
And those gallants who gallop in front,
So I think it's absurd that there's hardly a word
About us at the **back** of the hunt.

For remember, you thrusters, fence, hedge and wall busters,
Though the fences you jump may be higher,
We arrive at the trot and, as likely as not,
We find nothing much left but the wire.

At the first Tally Ho! away you all go
In pursuit of the hounds and the horn,
But we're in a crowd and the gossip's so loud
That we don't even notice you've gone.

"What a party last night!" "Didn't Sue look a sight?"
"I hear Marge let down more than her hair . . ."
"Did you hear what Lucille did to Tom in the reel?"
"Why's that chap got his hat in the air?"

Led by fat farmer Bob on his sturdy welsh cob
We all surge through a broken down gap,
Then we're stuck in a gate with a few who've come late
To avoid being caught for a cap.

Red ribbons abound, an unfortunate hound
Gets kicked and then dashes off squeaking.
Shouts old General Geoff, who is almost stone deaf
And whose horse kicked the hound. "They're speaking!"

The D.C., Lady Joan, is surrounded by ponies,
Which makes it quite hard to get past her,
And two bright young sparks, jumping hedges for larks
Are sent home by a furious Master.

There are one or two girls wearing earrings and pearls
And one very buxom young maiden
Wearing breeches so tight that, when seen in good light,
They appear — from behind — to be sprayed on.

With a bandage and boot on each leg and each foot
Is a group just along for the ride;
Never out of a walk, they do nothing but talk
And then go home at two — qualified.

Then we all get a fright when there comes into sight
First the fox, then the hounds — There's dismay
For a minute or two, till the field gallops through.
It is US who are showing the way.

Once again, far behind, we decide we will find
An inn, for we all have a thirst:
There we're joined for a drink by a man dressed in pink
Who had never got over the first.

So, you chaps out in front, have a jolly good hunt
And forget about those of us who
Are content just to hack in a crowd at the back —
Chacun as they say, à son goût.

Drawings by John Tickner

See Ho!

A merry sight the beaglers are,
With hounds and huntsman ranging far.
The woods and hills throw back the sounds
Of horn and music of the hounds
                    when beagling.

To follow hounds and hunt the hare
Of feet you only need a pair.
Their age no matter, man and boy
Can walk or run and both enjoy
                    their beagling.

Dukes and dustmen, men of riches,
Men who mend the council ditches,
Without a horse or rod or gun,
They one and all enjoy the fun
                    of beagling.

When, after several years of this,
Rheumatic pains reduce the bliss,
Don't give it up, for here's a thought
How you can still enjoy the sport
                    of beagling.

When panting far behind, alone,
Take heart! For reasons quite unknown,
The hare, her mind on other things,
When chased will often run in rings
                    round beagling.

So if, through age or lacking puff,
You feel that you have had enough
But still desire to view the chase,
You may, from some superior place,
                    watch beagling.

As round and round the hunters go,
Just sit and watch them down below,
Imbibing whisky from a flask,
One wonders — what more could one ask
                    of beagling?

Then, if by chance the chase moves on
And from one's view the hunt has gone,
The nearest inn's not far to walk
And later there they'll sing and talk
                    of beagling.

So, whether you prefer to run,
Or walk, or sit, you'll find it's fun.
A hare's afoot, they cry: "See Ho!"
There is no finer sport, I know,
                    than beagling.

Illustrated by John Tickner

Deposit Account

Though logs are talked of, if at all,
As easy things off which to fall,
I can't, myself, dispute the ease
With which one falls from prone, dead trees;
Since I am not a lumberjack
I practise off a horse's back.

Through front and back and both side doors
I make my exits. Newton's laws
Dictate that, parted from my horse,
I gravitate with fearful force.
Each year increasing age and weight
Accelerate my earthbound rate.

I've fallen now in every way
And even five times in one day.
Once, too well primed with stirrup cup,
I even fell, not down, but UP —
My horse and I being torn asunder
By branches he (not I) went under.

Once, mounted and about to greet
The Master at his own lawn meet,
I wished to God I'd not been born —
My horse lay down upon the lawn;
Beneath my horse one foot was caught,
I said, "Good day" and spilled my port.

If at a jump we take a flier,
My horse goes high, but I go higher;
On coming down, there is, alas!
No horse below me — only grass.
I lie there like a grounded Boeing,
While, far away, my horse keeps going.

Each buck, refusal, running out,
Each sudden shy or turn about
Ensures that I'm propelled once more
Through one or other open door,
Thus ending almost every ride
With hurt to more than just my pride.

An arm, a leg, a silk top hat,
(One bruised, one bent, one squashed quite flat)
Bear witness to my downward trend;
I ask myself, "Where will it end?"
It can't go on! Should I, perhaps,
Try using glue or safety straps?

Drawings by John Tickner

A Nip in the Air

Christmas Day celebrated and whole families sated
On a diet of turkey and stuffing
(Not to mention the port) — at the Boxing Day sport
There'll be plenty of huffing and puffing.

My horse stifles a groan, for I've put on a stone;
A quick dram, to the Meet at eleven.
There's a crowd in the square, stirrup cups everywhere —
By the time we move off I've had seven.

The effect of the drink is to make fences shrink;
We jump four on the way to the draw,
Where, there being a pause, to a round of applause,
Someone passes the port — "Vive le Sport!"

Before there's a view we all sample drambuie
And a nip from a flask of sloe gin,
Then a rum is knocked back and quick whisky mac
And my head is beginning to spin.

The adrenalin flows as away the hunt goes
Over fences not four inches high;
A check and I'm handy when out comes the brandy,
One more jump — Oops, I'm off! There's a cry . . .

"Hey, wake up, you old fool! You are starting to drool,
All that food and then too much to drink.
It's nearly 6.30, your boots are still dirty . . .
Good grief! I've been dreaming — I think.

Drawings by John Tickner

Phoxes and Feasants
A Brush with the Law

This is the tale of old Sir Dan,
A baronet and hunting man,
And of Jack who lived next door
And by his shooting set great store.
Jack's syndicate were quite determined
That their shoot should be de-vermined.
They shot the fox and were not sorry,
Whereas Sir Dan revered his quarry.

And then one day, the story goes,
These sportsmen really came to blows —
It happened when the scent was good
And hounds ran straight through Jack's best wood.
The pheasants scattered, spoiled the drive,
The fox (alas!) did not survive.
Sir Dan rode up, said Jack, "Don't rush!
I've shot your fox and here's the brush."

Sir Dan, quite miffed, then raised his whip
And angrily at Jack let rip.
Jack dodged and (not to be outdone)
Reloaded and discharged his gun.
Sad ending to a day of sport,
The matter finished up in court.
The magistrate who heard their tale
Promptly sent them both to jail.

I'm glad to say they made amends
In prison and became great friends.
I'm also happy to report
A common interest in sport
Made both see sense and they agreed
That, from the day when they were freed,
Each would forget his past disgrace
And share the pleasures of the chase.

Sir Dan now sometimes helps to beat
And Jack goes hunting on his feet —
Finding out to his surprise
How hounds can often help birds rise
And that the presence of a fox
Is not too harmful to his stocks.
**The hounds their quarry now pursue
And pheasants fly where fists once flew.**

Drawings by John Tickner.

Shooting and Stalking

SOME GLORIOUS FAILURES

The success of gossip writers depends largely on their having larders well stocked with juicy titbits, from which they can select suitable morsels for the daily delectation of their readers. Thus, over coffee and cornflakes, one is able to satisfy one's appetite for the affairs and affaires of the rich and titled.

While most of such writings are produced on a day-to-day basis, they are punctuated with great relish by a number of annual events, for which special sections of the columnists' larders are reserved. No section is better stocked with well chewed clichés than that marked August 12. Every year the same old truisms — and the same old falsisms, for that matter — are dutifully trotted out. The date is never anything but glorious and the moors continue to reverberate to the crash of rifle fire, etc, etc.

Thus it is that the impression is widely held of grouse

moors teeming with senior officials of the Conservative Party and the higher echelons of the aristocracy, with as many multi-millionaires as possible squeezed into any butts not already occupied by members of the first two categories. With the assistance of a pair of best British guns each, these gentlemen will soon be speeding thousands of grouse carcasses to the premier restaurants of the world.

Nor does responsibility for the presentation of this quaint and totally inaccurate picture, I regret, lie solely with the gossip writers. Not long ago I read a piece by a columnist on animal affairs (who should know better) in a daily paper (which should also know better) which referred to August 12 as "the day when it becomes legitimate for millionaires to slaughter grouse". How evocative is that word "slaughter" and how beloved it is of quasi-conservationists and others hell-bent on the destruction of field sports.

But, enough of philosophising! The moor on which I have been lucky enough to spend the opening days of the last few grouse seasons is not one of those frequented by Rolls-Roycefuls of shipping magnates. I have yet to hear an election address being practised in the next butt and the chance of seeing the glitter of sunlight reflected in a ducal coronet is, I would have thought, remote in the extreme. There is, mind you, good reason for this lack of noble patronage.

I can well remember (indeed, who could forget?) the first drive of the very first season. When we had reached the moor, after a hair-raising ride up a track that was only barely navigable, our eyes feasted themselves on a veritable wealth of healthy heather and we leapt from the Land-Rovers in high spirits. The talk at lower levels had all been about many years of neglect leading to poor prospects, but this was forgotten in a purple haze of optimism. With that much heather, there had to be grouse about.

The draw for places was made and we settled into our respective butts with eager expectancy. While it is true to say that all branches of field sports involve a period of waiting and require a high degree of patience in the participants — whether they be fishermen, hunters or wildfowlers — there is none that I know to compare with the nerve tingling suspense of waiting for the first covey of grouse to appear. This was a particularly long drive and time marched on leaden feet.

Suddenly and with an unexpectedness that brought instant alertness, there came a shout. There are other months of the year and other places far removed from a grouse moor when and where I would have been delighted to hear that yell. It was, in fact, a holloa and over the moor with a graceful lolloping stride came a beautiful golden-coloured fox. It was followed at intervals by other members of the same family. Not a bird came forward, unless you count the crows which, with contented smiles on their faces after a surfeit of grouse chicks and eggs, passed in a steady stream like over-fed diners leaving a restaurant at closing time. The drive concluded with a rather bemused flock of black-faced sheep being shepherded past the butts by the beaters.

The second, return drive was virtually a carbon copy of the first. Charles James and family were once again the first to appear, hastened on their way this time by an exasperated gentleman in number eight butt, who seized the chance to discharge his weapon for the first time that day. Only the crows were absent, possibly digesting their illgotten gains over the corvine equivalent of a decanter of port in a place undisturbed by the intrusions of man. Panting a bit by this time, the sheep made the return journey through the butts. I swear one old ram shook his head sadly at me as he passed by.

Succeeding drives were little more successful than the first two and the day's bag, towards which, incidentally, I did not contribute, was minimal.

The following day, which had been set aside for walking up, promised to be a real scorcher. The sun shone out of a cloudless sky, birds twittered in the trees and, by the time we had finished breakfast, a shimmering heat haze was rising from the hills opposite. I felt dreadful. The previous evening, what with a unanimous desire to wash away the day's woes and a lengthy discussion of the morrow's plans, the profits of a number of distilleries had been considerably enhanced. By closing time the prospect of a day's walk after grouse had held no more terrors than that of a post-prandial stroll round St. James's Park.

Now it was different. The moment of starting on a 20-mile slog through a bog-ridden, heather-filled sauna, carrying a gun, game-bag and hangover was upon us. The reality was, if possible, worse than the expectation.

Many years ago an ungrateful Air Ministry saw fit to despatch me to a part of the world where a gentleman with the unlikely title of the Imam of Oman was, for some reason best known to himself, disputing the ownership of a particularly unattractive piece of desert with the Sultan of Muscat and Oman. On one occasion during the campaign in which I found myself involved, I also found myself alone in the desert in a Land-Rover with a leaking radiator, on a day when the shade temperature passed the 130 degrees Fahrenheit mark. My distress then was never matched again until that day on top of a grouse moor.

The only member of the party who was not noticeably suffering from the heat was Sweep, a flat-coated retriever belonging to my host. Under other circumstances Sweep's turn of speed and incredible stamina might have been attributes to admire. As it was, he ensured that the few grouse not lying prostrate from heat became airborne anything up to half a mile ahead. Occasionally another, alarmed by the infuriated shouts emanating from Sweep's owner, also took flight well out of shot. Remarkably, we did each manage to get a bird or two — and I mean that literally. Some got one and others got two.

And so two memorable days came to a hot and sticky ending. I would like to be able to report that things were much better the following year. Sadly, I am unable to do so. True, the ranks of predators had noticeably thinned, but the extra grouse resulting from this reduction were blown away by gales of wind on the driving day and escaped virtually unscathed.

As the wind swept the moor on the first day, so Sweep swept it on the second. A year older maybe, but not one bit less energetic and, if anything, a shade more deaf to his master's loud and frequent requests for his immediate return. Still, we did manage to collect a few brace before returning, tired but reasonably happy, to base camp.

Succeeding years did not bring any noticeable increase in the bags, but those first two days of the grouse season remain among my fondest sporting memories. I only regret the absence of some of those gossip-writers to share them with us. It is a year or two since I last traversed that moor, though perhaps, one day, I may be lucky enough to do so again. That may well depend on whether the man responsible for it all reads these words, for I cannot leave the moor without providing a pen picture of his remarkable attributes. In order to avoid the Organiser being pestered with requests to be put on the waiting list for membership of this unique sporting estate, I will not use his real name — let me call him Brian James. Should it become necessary during the course of my subsequent narrative to mention individuals, I will refer to them as Peter, Tony, Fred, Tommy, James, Ted, Geoff or any other name that comes to mind. Thus will I preserve the anonimity both of the shoot and the participants.

Before we make the journey to the top, first I must acquaint you with the Boss. Brian — or B.J. as we know him — is a man to be listened to very carefully. For a start he is a prophet of extreme, nay uncanny, accuracy. How often have I heard him say, "There should be a bird or two here" as we line up before a chunk of the old blooming purple. To give oneself such a tiny margin of error in prediction is a sign of amazing self-confidence which, in the event, has always been fully justified. In good seasons there has indeed been a brace in the area depicted. In less favoured years there has been but a singleton.

Then again, he is an inveterate planner who, having made a plan, sticks rigidly to it — for anything up to five minutes. While the initial plan is always announced to the entire company, only a privileged few are entrusted with subsequent alterations. The bland look on B.J.'s face when the inevitable chaos ensues is something to behold.

Alas, his dog Sweep is no more, but there was a worthy successor, equally capable of clearing a moor of anything that can move. Nor has his owner seen fit to equip him with the hearing aid he so obviously needs. One of the great sights of the early season is B.J., office-bound during most of the year and not by any measure in the Steve Cram class, bounding through the heather when some extraordinarily stupid bird has failed to leave its haven early enough and been downed. The race to retrieve something more than a feather, foot, or part of a beak has been known to bring a tear to the eye of even the most hardened sportsman. The dog's name, by the way, was Tory and I am still not sure if it was named after the party which swept all before it, or was an abbreviation of Victoria, in tribute to those who had seen their best efforts reduced to a soggy heap of feathers and said they were "not amused".

Over the years, B.J. has so improved his driving technique and navigational powers that there is no longer the wonderful thrill and sense of tremendous relief there once was in arriving at the planned destination at the top of the hill. However, the "Sharp at nine start" is still the old move-off at around 9.45 it has always been and it is still mid-morning before we arrive at the actual starting point — incidentally, exactly twelve inches short of a mountain.

On the way up, wildlife sightings had been confined to a buzzard, two plover, a kestrel and considerable numbers of crows. In spite of this, we set off on the first walk with the familiar "There should be a bird or two here" ringing in our ears. Nevertheless, apart from a few wheezings, the only sounds heard for some time came from the occasional knee joint going off with a loud report, causing the odd passing crow to flinch visibly. Eventually a bird rises, is shot at extreme range and, although it falls a long way on down the hill, the sounds of Tory's first meal of the day blend with B.J.'s anguished cries and come drifting back to us on the north westerly breeze.

I must be fair. Had I shot the one I fired at, the bag at lunchtime would have been doubled. When I say 'lunch-time', I mean the hour at which most civilised people enjoy their midday meal. B.J. had other ideas. "There will," he announced firmly, "be plenty of time for another walk before lunch." And maybe there would have been, had the planned transport ferry service gone according to plan. By the time we were once again grinding to the top, it was difficult to distinguish the rumbles of an engine in low ratio bottom gear from those emanating from my stomach. Remarkably, four birds were added to the bag during the next spell, immediately after which we were ordered to re-embus. I disobeyed orders by snatching a bun from my basket at this point.

The meal, when finally taken, was a convivial affair, enlivened by the double report of a brace of champagne corks going skywards, again causing consternation among the attendant crows. The liquid celebration of The Twelfth was thanks to a guest and it was in good heart that we prepared for what I will term the afternoon, for want of a better word — noon having long since passed.

One of those sudden changes of plan to which I referred earlier now took place. As quietly as possible B.J. announced that, from henceforward, we would number from left to right, the reverse of the previously agreed system. This meant that the right hand gun would walk two miles along a reasonable path while the remainder struggled through deep heather, steep-sided gills and quaking bogs, though I am certain that B.J. himself being drawn number eight had nothing to do with the change. It also meant that I would have to shout loudly to my left instead of right, Tommy, my next door gun, being a little hard of hearing. He had also spent the previous night drying corn and, during pauses, was apt to fall asleep. My efforts to arouse him usually met with little success. There were some snipe about and, forgetful of the change, I subjected Fred (who was now on my right and whose hearing is perfect) to some very loud bellows indeed when they arose. It later transpired that Tommy thought they were not in season anyway.

The bag had now risen to nine. This fact and the rapid approach of opening time in the hostelry far below were taken into account when the decision to call it a day was made at the end of this perambulation. We collapsed thankfully, once again to await the cars that would take us down to that first delicious pint. I was, if you will excuse the phrase, completely knackered. I must confess, though, to a certain feeling of smug self-satisfaction that my lower limbs had managed to support my overweight torso in conditions to which they were unaccustomed, that is until I saw, rounding a nearby knoll, a limping, diminutive figure, knapsack on back, ancient in the extreme and supported by two sticks. "What a lovely day," I said by way of greeting and, supposing him to have been transported to our lofty perch, "How did you get up here?" "I walked," he replied. It was obvious that he suffered from a deformity in one foot and further questioning elicited the facts that he had walked up from the town a few miles distant and was 83 years old. Furthermore, he fully intended returning by a longer and even more precipitous route. I felt rather humble.

Oh yes, I almost forgot to mention that a crow, possibly mistaking the somnolent Tommy for a corpse, approached too close to the line at one stage and duly paid the penalty. Included under various it brought the bag up into double figures. Now that was something to celebrate.

EGYPTIAN DUCK

The first Jumbo I ever saw on a runway was not packed with more than 300 tourists; it was large, grey, pachydermatous, accompanied by about twenty of its fellows and had to be shepherded away by Air Traffic Control before I could effect a landing. I believe that the runway concerned no longer consists of the local soil, nor is it lined, as it often was, by very tall, stark naked natives of the most extraordinary physical proportions, on the exact details of which there is no need to dwell here. It, the runway that is, now extends for about two miles, is made of concrete and the elephants have long since departed.

From the foregoing you will have gathered that the period of which I write is not in the immediate past. It was not that long ago; it was, in fact, barely forty years ago.

I was, at the time, based in Egypt with a ground attack fighter squadron and our sphere of influence included the Sudan, wherein dwelt the elephants. On our return to Egypt, I was delighted to find that I, though a mere Pilot Officer (the lowest of the low, in case you are not familiar with Royal Air Force ranks), had qualified for a day's duck shooting with the Embassy Shoot. This piece of information may not cause you any surprise, but I can assure you that the lowest Army rank normally to qualify for this splendid affair was full Colonel — and there were not too many of them either. My good fortune lay in the fact that there happened to be a dearth of sporting RAF officers in the Canal Zone at the time.

The venue for the shoot was a marshy area, to the left and up a bit on the map from Tel el Kebir, itself a fairly godforsaken spot. Weekly, during the season, two parties set out towards what for duckshooters, but no one else, was a truly delectable spot. One party, headed by the ambassadorial Rolls, came from the west, the other, trailing in the dust left by the G.O.C.'s Humber, came from Ismailia.

As befitted my lowly position, I found myself in the rearmost Jeep of the westbound convoy, struggling to maintain contact, first in the dark and later through clouds of billowing sand. When we finally arrived, there was no drawing for places, which were allocated strictly according to rank. I therefore had an extremely long walk to my hide which turned out to be, by any standards, a very luxurious edifice, with a floor of firm boards raised above the water and surrounded by well bound reeds. The snag to this splendid appointment was having to share it with a filthy, evil-smelling wallah who had been deputed as my bearer for the day; yes, there was an underling, but his task was to retrieve, spending his time between successful shots standing up to his waist in water some distance away.

The signal for the start of the shoot was the firing of a cannon mounted on a boat in the lake which formed the centre of the marsh. Nowadays the same sound would doubtless send several flights of supersonic fighter aircraft airward, but in this case it caused several thousand ducks to become airborne. Immediately a furious fusillade broke out from the butts in the favoured central positions. It was some time before my first chance came and, in the meantime, I had to suffer the unwelcome attentions of my appointed assistant. In addition to the already mentioned smell, a continual coughing, interspersed with the occasional ill-directed spit, came from him. A further distraction was his incessant demands for "ceegareets" and his obvious designs on my cartridge bag did nothing to help my concentration. I therefore missed my first few chances at duck, but eventually started taking a few shots. As soon as the first success was registered, assistant No2, galabeer awash, came splashing out to retrieve, thereby effectively scaring away every duck within sight, of which by then there was a considerable number.

For the next three hours, flights of duck, expletions of betel juice from between two blackened teeth onto my feet and the weird cavortings of my retriever, alternated in roughly equal proportions. Sharp at midday shooting ceased and the time had come for me to dispense 'bakhshish' — a tip — to my two companions, I can hardly call them helpers. Custom dictated that I donated the lot to No1, with whom I had unwillingly shared my butt for three hours and who had done nothing to increase my enjoyment of the day. I am absolutely certain that No2 saw nothing of it — and he at least had tried.

The long walk back — No2 encumbered with the bag, myself with gun and cartridge bag, neither of which I trusted with No1 — terminated with our arrival at a numbered peg, alongside which the results of one's efforts had to be deposited for all to see. Such had been the barrage from the hides nearest the centre, that I fully expected my own modest tally to cause some merriment. Cartridges were, in those days, extremely cheap. Even so, I was amazed (and not asked again) to find that I had shot more than some of those in the favoured places — and I am not a very good shot.

There was another, less illustrious, shoot, not far removed from the Embassy Shoot. This was known as the B.T.E. (British Troops in Egypt) Shoot. Again to my surprise I found myself offered a place. Shooting times being different, it was considered necessary for this occasion to spend the night prior to shooting in a tented encampment adjacent to the following morning's sport. Suitably equipped, as I thought, for a day's sport, I proceeded thither. I was only slightly alarmed to find myself being conducted to an immaculate tent by an equally immaculate batman and to be informed that dinner was to be served at 8p.m. in the mess tent. That my alarm increased considerably on my entry to said tent at the appointed hour will be understood when I tell you that

I was ushered in by a gloved and white-jacketed steward towards a dinner-jacketed Brigadier (I was by then a Flying Officer) and the smartest part of my apparel was an off-white rollneck sweater.

Worse was to follow. The seating arrangements somehow contrived to place me opposite to the Brigadier's personal guest, a large floribund man, my instant dislike of whom I managed to conceal during the meal by maintaining a discreet silence. Throughout dinner, the conversation centred around the relative merits of various types of cartridges and, in order to remain as unobtrusive as possible, I avoided joining in by imbibing quantities of wine which circulated at frequent intervals. The port was my undoing. It was while I was sipping my third — or was it my fourth? — glass, that the Brigadier's guest, who had just proclaimed loudly that his cartridges were specially shipped to him by a very well known London gunmaker, leant towards me and asked what cartridges I favoured.

One less glass and a modicum of discretion would have produced a different answer. As it was I told the truth.

"Trap-shooting cartridges," I replied, for they were virtually free at the time.

There was what can best be described as a sort of 'Harrumph' from the other side of the table, conversation changed to other matters and, shortly afterwards, I chose a suitable moment to retire.

The procedure the following day was roughly the same as on the Embassy Shoot, only on a less extravagant scale. To my intense relief I found that I was not allocated any native assistants so I proceeded to my far flung post unaccompanied. This in turn resulted in my having to return to the central point carrying my own, consequently larger, share of the spoils. Modesty, not to mention a poor memory, prevents me from telling you what my bag was. My recollection is entirely clear however, that opposite the numbered peg of the gentleman sitting across the table from me the night before, was lying a single, rather bedraggled teal.

Perhaps it was as well that the distance I had to travel to register my tally was sufficient to allow the departure of the more senior members before I arrived on the scene. Otherwise I might have said something else I regretted.

OVER THE HILL

Like all sports, stalking has its own terminology which it behoves the beginner to learn if he is to avoid mistakes which might spoil his enjoyment. In the case of Highland stalking, the strange new words are the harder to comprehend, often being spoken out of the corner of the mouth in a thick Scottish accent and usually into the teeth of a gale.

Here, then, is a short glossary of some of the terms, the interpretation of which I learned through hard experience:

Hill
A precipitous mountain, the top of which is invariably hidden by cloud.

Wee bit of a breeze
A gale

Mist (pronounced must)
When you can see absolutely nothing

Missed (pronounced must)
Your eyes need testing

Path

A Scottish joke word for the route you take up the hill

Piece

A packed lunch carried in the pocket which, after a stalk, is inextricably mixed with the other contents and usually contains at least one bullet

Gralloch

What is removed from a dead stag just as you were about to start on your piece

Drag

Pulling a stag's carcase over almost impassable ground (N.B. It has nothing to do with Danny la Rue in a tartan frock)

Monarch

A stag (cf. Landseer's glen)

Muttony monarch

A stag which, on closer inspection, turns out to be a sheep

Damned grouse

An unsporting bird that jumps up and spoils a stalk

Face (1)

The side of a hill

Face (2)

That which, when exposed to Face (1), clears it of deer

The Rifle

Not, as you might imagine, a weapon, but the person who pulls the trigger. The title 'Stalker' is reserved for the chap who knows what he is doing

Forest

A very large tract of land entirely devoid of trees

Donald

Due to a shortage of christian names in Scotland, most of the stalkers, pony boys, ponies and probably many of the stags all have the same name. In my case it was Donald, you may find a preponderance of Willies, Ewans or Iains

Foot

Five toes and a heel held together by blisters

For my first attempt at stalking, preceded by the inevitable Donald, I was led up the sort of slope I consider suitable only for mountain goats, extremely fit Sherpas or, possibly, for me in a funicular. It was not long before my legs, unaccustomed to near vertical progression, started to complain and my lungs, no doubt astonished by sudden inrushes of Highland air, wheezed painfully. Frequent dizzy spells beset me. Only the sight of Donald's remorselessly lifting boots kept me going.

During the climb one's hopes are continually raised by apparently being able to see the summit not far ahead. Having reached this goal, it can then be seen that there is another 'summit' ahead, then another and another. Like the oasis in a mirage, it retreats before one. At last we did reach the top after an ascent that Donald described as 'quite a nice wee climb'. There was still quite a way to go but, with the going considerably easier, it was possible to enjoy the surroundings.

From the heather, grouse, singly and in coveys, continually jumped — their 'go-back, go-back, back, back' seeming to voice their resentment at our intrusion. Ptarmigan, still in summer plumage, golden plover and the odd snipe could also be seen. Once, a sudden familiar sound had me scanning the sky keenly until I spotted a skein of greylag geese tumbling out of the clouds and arguing loudly about which direction they should take. Their sudden appearance startled a distant party of deer into panicky flight. A little later we had a superb view of a golden eagle as it swept past on fixed wings, causing Donald to remark: "I wouldna mind becoming one of those in my next life." Somewhere beneath that leathery exterior beat a romantic's heart.

Wildfowlers and fishermen in particular will know what I mean when I say that the time spent actually in close pursuit of one's quarry is minimal compared with that spent in preparation and in just waiting. Indeed, this applies to most field sports, none more than stalking. The long climb and the subsequent search for a suitable beast can take several hours, the actual stalk may be of only a few minutes duration, or, as in the case of my first stag, no time at all.

A number of watchful hinds were between the possible

target Donald had spotted and ourselves and it was while trying to circumnavigate these sentinels that I suddenly found myself eyeball to eyeball with one. I had not earlier appreciated that the route Donald had chosen, while perfectly adequate to conceal his diminutive self, left a portion of my much larger frame exposed.

"Whissht!" I whispered as I sank to the ground. At least 'whissht' (a useful Scottish alarm signal I had picked up) was what I meant to say, but my false teeth slipped and it came out as more of a 'phlutt'. Anyway it had the desired effect.

"What was it?" asked Donald, probably thinking I needed yet another stop to rest my limbs.

"There's a large hind just ahead," I replied in a whisper, having readjusted my dentures.

"Damn," muttered Donald, "We'd better bide a wee, before trying to move round her."

Having bided whatever constitutes a wee, Donald inched himself up the bank, spent a moment or two peering over the top and then returned in a state of great excitement.

"That's nae heend, mon, it's a ruddy great hummel."

My heart sank. A 'hummel', to a chap with visions of a many-pointed hatrack in the hall, is about as popular as a bald man in a hairdressers — and equally rare. It is, in fact a hornless stag, which must speedily be disposed of before it produces progeny of the same ilk. All I had to do was move a yard or two with reasonable care and Donald was ecstatic at the result of my first shot at a stag. There were to be no more chances that day and, somewhat despondently, legs aching and barely able to support me, I was back in the Lodge.

However, the restorative effects of a glass or two of Scotland's favourite tipple are remarkable. In no time at all, I was boring everyone to death with highly exaggerated accounts of my achievement. They must have been mightily relieved when I finally retired to bed flushed, I have to admit, not only with success.

On waking the next morning I appreciated for the first time what the expression 'he's gone over the hill' really means. I was there. I felt very old indeed, every limb throbbed with pain and the act of getting out of bed required quite an effort. Dressing and pulling socks over badly blistered feet was agony and, as for donning my boots . . . printable words fail me. All this had to be borne because that day there was another hill to climb and, perhaps, another stag to be shot.

Thankfully, the climb was less severe, although, due to the injuries I had sustained the day before, no less painful. Remarkably too, the Stalker allocated to me was not only called Donald but was female. No matter, the result was exactly the same. I shot another hummel.

My account of the day's proceedings received noticeably greater respect that evening. I was, after all, on my way to becoming Scotland's greatest expert on hornless stag shooting. We had been joined by the ducal Laird who, after expressing initial incredulity, consulted the record books. These confirmed that hummels had only rarely been seen in the forest, still less shot, over many years.

Only the presence of a witness, yet another Donald, allows me to relate that, on alighting from the Land Rover at the head of the glen on the third morning, I put up my fieldglasses and sharply into focus came — a hummel. The only reason my name does not appear in the *Guinness Book of Records* is because that one managed to outmanoeuvre us.

I would like to take my hat off to those whose expertise at stalking has been rewarded by visible and tangible results. The trouble is, I still have nowhere to hang it.

Hi Lost!

Oh, the dogs on our shoot! "Will you come here, you brute!"
You can hear them shout all down the line.
Untrained and unruly, I promise you truly
That the only exception is mine.

There's old Colonel Jack, swearing, flat on his back
With his gun pointing up in the air.
You can hear how he felt when, attached to his belt,
His young labrador spotted a hare.

Dick's bird hits the ground, four dogs make a bound
And arrive on the scene all together.
They divide it in three and, from what I can see,
Dick's dog brings him back just one feather.

That spaniel of Joe's has a terrible nose,
A fact which accounts for the reason
Why he mutters rude words as he looks for his birds
— His dog hasn't found one all season.

"Get away from my bitch!" That's Fred's springer which,
(Apart from being too over-sexed)
Getting quite overwrought, drops each bird that it's caught
Before dashing straight on to the next.

Bob's not been too clever and used as a tether
His cartridge bag fixed to a stake.
When a rabbit went past, his dog took off fast
With his bag — now they're both in the lake.

I cannot believe a worse golden retriever
Exists than the one owned by Jones.
The only sound heard when it picks up a bird
Is a horrible crunching of bones.

But even that's better than Charlie's red setter,
Which is really the worst of the bunch.
After eating a pheasant, it did something unpleasant
While we all sat around having lunch.

Quite deaf to Jane's yell, like a bat out of hell
Goes her flat-coated dog being active
In pursuit of a runner and, though Jane is a stunner,
Her dog I find far from attractive.

No, you cannot dispute that the dogs on our shoot
Are the worst ever seen in a line.
Look, there goes one now and it's chasing a cow,
Disgraceful! Good gracious, it's mine!

Drawings by John Tickner

Covert Charge

With costs ever steeper, the life of a Keeper —
It is not what it was, I'm afraid.
Now, instead of some earls and their debutante girls,
We have eight paying guns, all in trade.

Number one gun this week, who's in shipping and Greek,
Fires a hundred and twenty-three times.
All he gets for his trouble is a curious double
Of a dog and a beater called Grimes.

The young man number two has got something to do
With the City and comes here by air.
Although I have heard he has shares in James Purdey,
In the bag he does **not** have a share.

There's a butcher at three and it's quite plain to see
That he's not been before to a shoot.
He has just blown to bits a hen thrush and two tits
And then carved up a stationary coot.

Next to him is a brewer who, at lunch, had no fewer
Than five gins, which he drank much too quick.
In the best place at four, he is starting to snore
When he hiccoughs and falls off his stick.

Not one bird takes a dive as they pour over five,
Not a shot does the fishmonger fire.
A crab in his diet has caused some disquiet
And has made him discreetly retire.

Just beyond those two ricks is a tailor, at six,
Who is neatly turned out in bespoke.
Having opened his score with a shot in the straw,
There's a **baa!** when he lets off his choke.

A distiller from Fife, drawn seven, has a wife
Who is Spanish and all through the drive,
When he raises his gun, shouts "You no shoot zat one!
He's so preety, I like heem alive."

With a pump gun at eight's an oil man from the States,
Wearing clothes such as I've never seen.
At each bird that goes past there's a long drawn out blast,
When he empties a full magazine.

I am sorry to say, at the end of the day
When I lay out the bag on the ground,
Even counting poor Grimes and a bird shot ten times,
There is not quite enough to go round.

Drawing by John Tickner

The Furious Twelfth

There are many commuters and casual shooters
(Often not in the best state of health)
Pack their tweeds and plus fours and head north for the moors
On the eve of the 'Glorious' Twelfth.

Next day, muscles aching, they take their time making
Their way up the moorside until,
More dead than alive, at last they arrive
In their butts at the top of the hill.

Old Donald the keeper then plunges them deeper
In gloom, "Och, it's nai guid, I fear.
What with rain, snow and hail, the blight, drought and gale,
I doubt we'll see many this year."

The grouse fly so fast that the birds have gone past
Before most of the guns open fire.
Grouse shooting's an art which I, for my part,
Must admit I have yet to acquire.

Birds all down the line — "On your left! Yours! That's mine!"
Guns pointing in every direction.
Down the hill there's a yell, it's because a few pellets
Hit Hamish, who makes an objection.

Colonel Jack, in his butt, is doing his nut;
Purple faced he emits a loud roar,
As his dog, going spare in pursuit of a hare,
Puts every bird up on the moor.

There are plenty of birds but, to quote Donald's words
On the bag when expressing disgust,
"Is this all ye've got? Just look what ye've shot,
Compared with the burrds that ye mussed."

The bag is sent down on the first 'plane to Town,
Where for grouse (why not 'grouses' or 'grice'?)
They are willing to pay for birds shot that day
An exorbitant à la carte price.

Whose blood is not stirred by this singular bird,
Far more valued than pheasants and partridges?
As a target or meal, grouse are worth a great deal —
Not least to the makers of cartridges.

When it comes to the Twelfth, for the sake of your health,
Keep your head down or stay in your house,
Or you risk being shot, then, as likely as not,
You will have a legitimate grouse.

Drawings by John Tickner

Deer, Oh Dear!

I agree that a stag looks at home on a crag
In the forest of which he's a denizen.
*But his antlers look grand in **my** home as a stand*
For my hats — and I'm partial to venison.

Mind you, going stalking is not merely walking
Through heather, then lying down flat
And just firing a shot — I assure you it's not —
There is rather more to it than that.

If, like me, you're not fit, or habitually sit
In an office or watching T.V.,
Then stalking's a sport I suggest that you ought
To forget . . . Look what happened to me!

For a start there's the 'hill', which I climb up until
I'm on top of a very large mountain.
Where the 'mist' (fog to you) first erases the view
And then drenches us like a fountain.

My task's but a trifle for I am the 'Rifle',
With nothing to do but the firing;
It's the Stalker, of course, and the man with the horse
Who work — I just follow, perspiring.

"We'll just have a wee spy," I sink down with a sigh.
For I'm aching and starting to wilt.
(A 'wee spy' is a peer through the 'glass' for a deer,
***Not** a mini James Bond in a kilt).*

When we've sighted a beast, still to go there's at least
Half a mile, mostly flat on my tum,
While the burn water leaks through the top of my breeks,
Making parts of me frigidly numb.

I look over a 'hag' and line up on a stag,
But then — what a horrid surprise!
At le moment critique with the stock in my cheek.
From the heather two ramblers arise.

As the hill clears of deer, "They shuild no do that here,"
Says the Stalker, "We'll have to retire.
There'll be no stag today." So we three wend our way
To the Lodge and a dram by the fire.

"What a beautiful stand — don't those antlers look grand!"
(I've gone up in my neighbours' esteem).
"Yes, it makes a good show — it's a Royal, you know."
But, alas! it is all still a dream.

Drawings by John Tickner

Bird's-Eye View

THE VERY OLD PHEASANT

I'm a very old pheasant and the reason I'm present,
When most of my friends have been eaten,
Is I always remember, from the First of November,
*To **walk** when the coverts are beaten.*

BACK CHAT

Said the grouse to the ptarmigan. *"They're about to rearm again!*
Soon our hills will be filled with grouse beaters.
*So, I'll run or fly **back**, thus avoiding the flak,*
Not to mention intending grouse eaters."

GEE WHIZZ!

I am not very big and I fly zig-zag-zig —
A most fortunate habit because,
When you loose off a shot, it, more often than not,
Whizzes not where I is but I was.

EGGS-ASPERATION

Through the whole month of May, how we birds sing all day,
As we build with a feverish zest.
It's all right for cuckoos, but Blimey! just look who's
Laid a dirty great egg in my nest!

Drawings by Rodger McPhail

The Ten Deadly Sinners

10 jolly shooters were walking up in line,
When a bird that flew between them fell — and so did No. 9

9 jolly shooters went to climb a five-barred gate,
Where one of them, still loaded, cut the party down to eight.

8 jolly shooters were shooting down in Devon,
But a snapshot through a hedgerow, pruned the number
down to seven.

7 jolly shooters — then a woodcock jumps and flicks.
They missed the bird, but one of the guns got a charge
of No. 6.

6 jolly shooters, till one tripped and took a dive.
If his safety catch had been on 'SAFE', there might still be
more than five.

5 jolly shooters travelled, sat on bales of straw,
Till a pothole jarred a loaded gun — what luck! — the shot
missed four.

4 jolly shooters were reduced to only three
By a gun left fully loaded and leant against a tree.

3 jolly shooters, until a blocked choke barrel blew.
If he'd checked before he loaded —ah, well — that left two.

2 jolly shooters; till one held the other's gun,
"It's unloaded!" — but it wasn't — and that left just the one.

1 solitary shooter while out shooting had a drink.
He dropped his gun and that left none — there's a moral
here, I think.

Drawings by John Tickner

IT IS FUN TO GO OUT SHOOTING AND TO EXERCISE ONE'S SKILL,
BUT REMEMBER, WHEN YOU HOLD ONE, THAT A GUN'S DESIGNED TO KILL.
VERY SIMPLE, BUT ESSENTIAL, ARE THE SHOTGUN SHOOTING RULES;
THOSE WHO FAIL TO OBEY THEM — IF ALIVE— ARE LUCKY FOOLS.

Fishing

FISH, FLESH & FOUL

No-one, even by the wildest stretch of imagination, could classify me as an expert fisherman. The only knots that I can tie really efficiently are those that appear two or three inches from the end of my cast with a dismal and unfailing regularity. It was therefore with a fair degree of trepidation that I allowed myself to be persuaded into a night fishing expedition after sea-trout (or, as they are known in those parts, "sewin") in the River Towy in Carmarthenshire.

My host was one of the keenest fishermen alive and with the ability to transmit his enthusiasm to others. In no time at all he had rigged me out in a pair of waders, pressed a rod and net into my hands and we were off to the river down a pitch black, thickly wooded and very steep hill. Impeded as I was by waders which were too short for me, my progress was a lumbering, stumbling scramble punctuated by frequent stops every time my rod got caught in some unseen hazard. Eventually, however, we made it to the bank.

Lack of wind and the bright full moon made it possible

to see and hear fish jumping all over the place and it was with pleasurable anticipation that I gingerly eased myself into the water, the aim being to get far enough out to be able to cast right across the river. Everywhere around me fish were leaping from the water, the smaller ones with their tails aquiver producing a noise not unlike a drumming snipe. One big one, disdainful of my presence (he had, I must admit, little to fear) heaved himself out of the swift-flowing current almost at my elbow. His silvery body, flashed in the moonlight and he seemed to hang suspended in mid-air for a moment before dropping back with a resounding splash that drenched my face.

My technique, if that is not too daring a word to use, failed to produce anything to put into my net, although I did get a couple of nibbles. My total score that night added up to one hat, one left ear lobe, two vicious swipes on the back of the neck and several leaves off the far bank. At least the latter showed I was reaching the far side. In a mean sort of way, I was quite pleased to find that my host had only managed to catch one himself. After all, he was the expert and it would have been rude to outfish my host.

The return journey to the house was even more fraught with danger than the outward one. The moonlight by now was pale and the shadows deep. If you have ever tried walking uphill in a pair of waders that are too small, you will appreciate why I was quite pleased not to be carrying a heavy basket of fish. A forward and upward movement of the knee tightens the backside of the waders round one's own. This has the effect of snapping the foot down on the ground again which, in turn, brings the body sharply forward. It feels rather as though one is being manipulated by a very inept puppeteer on strings that have been cut to unequal lengths. After what seemed an age, we eventually regained the house where I fell thankfully into bed.

During my short stay in Wales, I was lucky enough to fit in another visit to the river, this time in daylight. Able at last to see where I was going, I strode out into the river, anxious to do better this time and bearing in mind the old Scottish adage "You'll no be catching any fush wi'out your fly in the water." My guide and mentor was giving me advice from the bank but my impatience and the rushing water carried his words out of earshot. The words "You ought to . . ." came faintly over the water before the river closed over my head as I stepped into a pool and sank without trace. I surfaced in time to hear ". . . .shallower a bit further down." Undeterred by a large section of the Towy swilling about in my waders, I started hopefully to drop my fly where I had been told and within a few minutes I had my first ever sea-trout in the net. Over-confidence caused me to lose several others, but I met with moderate success and a day later I ate my catch. The fish gave me as much pleasure in the eating as they had in the catching. The eating, however, took a great deal less time.

HERE COMES THE JUDGE!

The telling of a story about an event in Ireland is never easy. There are always so many diversifications, tributaries if you like, to the mainstream of the central tale. Nothing is ever simple and straightforward. So it was with the day of the first fish. It really began the day before, so that is where I, too, will begin.

We had been to Crossmolina, "The City" as it was called, and the centre of social life, to book Paddy as our ghillie for the following day. We called him Cross-eyed Paddy to distinguish him from others, of whom there was a considerable number bearing the same name. He was remarkable also for having only one visible tooth, a ferocious expression and several days' growth of stubble on his chin. These latter characteristics were, however, common to 30 or 40 other Paddies. Only our Paddy had the ability to affix you with a steely glare from one eye while the other scanned the lough, watched his boat or followed a pair of pretty legs down the street.

Booking Paddy was not so simple as it sounds. A regular inhabitant of all the many inns he was and, even when one hit off his line, the chase could be a long one. It was no good being in a hurry. "You'll be stopping for a quick one then?" or "Won't you he having a wee tincture with us?" and a story or two to be exchanged at each stopping place. "Did you not see the big salmon the

61

Father caught last Sunday? And him having it in the boat not an hour after celebrating mass. To be sure, the Lord was with him." Eventually Paddy was found ("Well, just a half I'd be enjoying") and arrangements were made for the following day ("Ah, seeing as how it's empty, I wouldn't be minding the other half, thank you very much") and we were able to return to our holiday home.

Arrived at our destination, we were surprised to see a car parked beside the caravan in which we were living at the time. To reach the caravan, parked at the edge of Lough Conn, one left "the tar" a mile or two outside Crossmolina and drove down a long, winding, pot-holed and narrow farm track, through several farm gates and a farmyard, before crossing three fields. It was not, therefore, a centre of great activity and our surprise at finding someone else there was understandable.

The owner of the car turned out to be a charming bank manager from County Sligo. He had found himself unexpectedly with time on his hands as the banks were on strike and had decided on a quick fishing holiday. With him was his friend, a draper from Cork, who had temporarily closed down his business because of a lack of power and lighting. This has been caused by a strike of the Electricity. It would have been churlish not to have asked them in for a drink.

The children were asleep when an hour or so, several drinks and many stories later, we heard shouts outside. We stumbled out into the gathering darkness to perceive, some 40 or 50 yards out on the lough, a figure standing up in a boat, the motor of which had obviously ceased to function. Across the water came a neat description of the man who built the motor followed by a pithy and entirely derogatory history of his ancestry. "Here," said the bank manager, "comes the judge." This was a correct forecast, for the man we towed in with his boat was, indeed, a retired judge who had a house a mile or so down the lough.

The caravan settled a little more heavily at its southern end as the judge squeezed in with the others. The bottle circulated with the stories and the night wore on. There was one brief interlude to replenish stores from the judge's house but finally the bottles and the stories had all dried up. The bank manager, the draper and the judge bade us farewell and we fell thankfully on to our bunks. It was half-past two.

Some time later I was aroused by a shout of "Snoring!" and a well-aimed cushion. "I was not," I exlaimed indignantly and, to prove my point, there came at that moment from underneath the caravan the most appalling noise. It was loud enough to wake even the children who had slept soundly through all the earlier disturbances. My first thought was that our learned friend, who if not actually intoxicated could hardly have qualified to be as sober as a judge, might have decided to spend the remainder of the night beneath us. A further eruption made me realise that no human being could possibly be responsible for such a horribly discordant sound. There was nothing for it but to investigate, while the rest of the family, doubtless with visions of the little people having an orgy not two feet beneath them, pulled the bedclothes higher over their faces.

I do not know who was the more surprised, the corncrake or I. Caught in the bright beam of the torch, beak agape to produce what to another corncrake may well be a very attractive noise, there he stood. Not for long though. With a cry of rage at this disturber of my night's rest, I set about him. I can admit now that there may have been a humorous aspect to the chase that ensued. At the time it was all deadly serious. Pyjamaed, gumbooted and dressing-gown flapping, my quarry was two fields away before I gave up the pursuit, secure in the knowledge that he was unlikely to return to a place where, even to a corncrake's limited intelligence, it must be obvious that his presence was not entirely welcome.

Paddy's arrival, later that morning, was not greeted with the rapture he might have expected. His appearance, stubble a day longer and tooth unbrushed, was hardly one to inspire confidence when he manifested himself at the door of the caravan. Prospects improved somewhat when I remembered that it was my wife, and not I, who had to do the work today. She had yet to catch her first fish and my job was to sit up in the front end keeping the children quiet and perhaps taking them on an exploration in one of the islands in the lough.

Conditions were by no means ideal. An icy wind had whipped up the surface so that little grey waves chased each other across the lough until they came slap, slap, against the side of the boat. Every now and again one, bolder than the rest, would jump over the edge and join the few inches of muddy water already swilling about in the bottom. It was not the best of days on which to be catching one's first fish.

But she kept at it, encouraged by a steady stream of almost unintelligible advice from Paddy. The children and I went off to investigate an island and to look for pirates and treasure. Alas, it seemed there were no pirates, treasure nor even fish to be found that day, for, when we re-embarked, nothing had been hauled aboard.

Then suddenly, all was changed. There was a quick jerk, a dipping line, a flurry of water and cries of "Pull him in! Pull him in!" Excited shouts accompanied the reeling in of the line until there, suspended in mid-air for all to see, was one of the smallest trout ever to be pulled out of the water. It would not have felt out of place in a dish of whitebait and how it had managed to swallow the fly I will never know. Paddy, however, rose quickly to the occasion. "You'll not," he said, "be throwing this one back. Not your first fish." With that he tapped it on the head as he deftly disengaged it from the hook. 'And besoides," he exclaimed, "it will be after making you a very foine bookmarker."

Current Affairs
(a salmon and trout association)

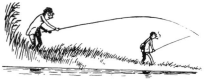

As a healthy young salmon, there's no question I am an
Unbelievably popular fish,
For I don't have a match as a wonderful catch
Or, regrettably, served as a dish.

Every day down our banks march the green-wellied ranks,
Casting hard at each fish as it passes.
As I look up I see the reflection of me
Keeping pace in their polaroid glasses.

I have travelled afar since my days as a parr
And much water's flowed under the bridge,
While a lot of my friends met unfortunate ends
In a tin or a freezer or fridge.

Now I've made it a rule, when I stop in a pool,
To examine the dangers about.
As the water gets low and I swim to and fro,
I'm advised by the resident trout . . .

"Smoking's bad for one's health, you must use all your stealth
If you don't wish to be a first course.
Do you know what they do? They squeeze lemon on you
Or, in my case, it's horseradish sauce.

"See that fly? No, don't grab it, through need, greed or habit,
Or an odd piscatorial whim.
You will have to submerge every fly-grabbing urge,
If you want to stay here in the swim.

"See that tiny fish flash? You must not make a dash
Without taking a long careful look,
For, like some of the flies, it may hide a surprise
In the shape of a very sharp hook.

"And, as for those ghillies, they give me the willies,
For they choose the most succulent flies.
Watch that one, he's canny, knows each rock and cranny
And the places where I like to rise."

That old trout saved my skin, I wave *"Thanks!"* with my fin
And, resuming my upriver dash,
I set off for the redds (sort of wet nuptial beds)
Where, with luck, things will go with a splash.

Drawings by John Tickner

Tight Lines!

In rivers, streams, canals and weirs,
In lakes and lochs, ponds, pools and meres,
From boats and beaches, punts and piers,
With flies and spinners, nets and spears,
In north and southern hemispheres —
He's fished for years and years and years.

But now, increasing age and gout
Have rendered safe from him the trout,
The salmon, grayling, bream and pike,
The tench, roach, rudd, perch, dace and like.
No more his prey the eel and chub —
It's US, the members of his club.

He waves his hands, his fingers twirl,
While demonstrating blood and turle.
For hours and hours we must endure
His endless talk of bait and lure,
Blue Charm, Dunkeld, Marlodge, Jock Scott
And flies whose names I long forgot.

With arms outstretched throughout the day,
He tells of fish that got away
And, after dinner, gaining strength,
Both fish and stories grow in length.
Impervious to our groans and snores,
Just like the Severn — HOW he bores!

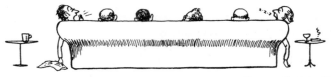

Illustrated by John Tickner

Country Life

The Country Seat

They were built like emporia in the reign of Victoria
In the castle, or manor, or grange,
With their seats made of wood, which have gamely withstood
Pressures greater than mere winds of change.

Boys with bats, balls, or oars, sportsmen sporting 12-bores
Gaze in rows from the walls on the sitter.
Draughts and damp old stone tiles mean today's stately piles
Suffer badly from cold that is bitter.

But, forget all the strain, pull the gleaming brass chain
(With a porcelain handle, no less),
And, released by a piston, from within a vast cistern
Comes a roar — and you're flushed with success.

Drawing by Rodger McPhail

Week in . . .

. . . Weak out

Hello, there! Nice to hear you — and have you time to speak?
Yes . . . nothing much has happened, just an average sort of week.
It was on the **Monday** morning that the veterinary came
In answer to our urgent call that Merrilegs was lame.

Then on **Tuesday**, after breakfast, both the dogs
                                              had disappeared
And, when they came to light again, it was worse than we
                                              had feared.
For our neighbours paid a visit and to greet them on our mat
Was a bloody little terrier; in our spaniel's mouth, their cat.

The hunter trials, on **Wednesday**, did not go frightfully well;
Four refusals, several run-outs and, when the pony fell,
The bridle broke, a shoe came off, the rider needed stitches
And stitches also needed to repair a pair of breeches.

Great excitement on the **Thursday**, for we had a new arrival,
When Grandad's gift, a puppy, joined the battle for survival.
First it chewed a pair of slippers, then ate half a Stilton cheese,
Regurgitated on a bed and gave the children fleas.

The sky was clear on **Friday**, sun shining on the pond.
But suddenly I noticed, up above and just beyond,
A slowly flapping heron and I shouted — much too late.
Now the pond's bereft of goldfish and the heron's overweight.

On the **Saturday** we hunted, but returned to disrepair;
A fox had had the chickens, there were feathers everywhere.
So eggs went off the menu, but an unexpected boost
To our much depleted livestock when the rabbit reproduced.

While at church on **Sunday** morning, first the puppy
                                        Grandad brought us
Upended, then ingested our revered and ancient tortoise.
Quite apart from upset children — predictably, they cried —
It did something simply ghastly to the wretched pup's inside.

It was early **Monday** morning that we called the vet again;
He attended to the puppy, I attended to the stain.
So sorry, I must stop now, I've just heard a fearful shriek.
I'll tell you who — or what — it was, when I telephone next week.

Drawings by John Tickner

HAY FEVER

Buying a much desired piece of land is exciting enough in itself. The prospect of a crop of hay from it, should the deal be concluded in time, added considerably to the thrill of an acquisition I once made.

As the date for completion approached, the frequency with which I took surreptitious peeps at the thickening crop increased. At the same time the adjoining few acres on which our horses grazed became increasingly bare of grass. The longing with which I gazed at the lush pasture soon to be mine was matched by that of the horses as, with ears pricked, they peered over the intervening fence like a group of mendicants staring through the window of a restaurant at the preparations for a gourmets' feast. Feverishly I patched and strengthened potential gaps, fearful lest the hoped for hay crop should vanish overnight in some nocturnal equine orgy.

No less feverish were my calculations as to the possible value of the succulent bales I could already visualise crammed to the rafters of my newly built storage space. No matter that wiser heads than mine shook warningly while their owners murmured about the difficulties of collecting hay in a climate such as ours. Hitherto, hay had been a commodity I had bought like any other, heedless of the processes by which it had been brought to a state of edibility. There was, I thought, no barrier between the gently waving grass and a veritable wealth of hay in my barn.

It all seemed so simple, £2 an acre for cutting, £1 an acre for turning and 9p a bale. Now, let's see — four and a half acres; that comes to £13.50 plus (say 400 bales) £36. Call it £50 which, at about 12p a bale, seems much better than shelling out a crispy oncer for a few mouthfuls of someone else's hay. Such blissful ignorance was due for a rude and early awakening.

The first inkling of possible disaster came while I was being conducted round the field of a farming neighbour on a tour of inspection during one of the few brief spells free from the almost incessant rain that descended throughout the early summer months. This inclement weather had been preceded by a period of intense drought during which the grass, starved of nourishment, had almost entirely failed to grow.

Here and there could be discerned a few wispy pieces of grass, some of it green but the majority verging on black, a hue that was reflected in the facial expression of my friend as he desultorily kicked the odd mouldy blade with a damp toe. Even to my inexperienced eye, the prospect of 400 bales of sweet smelling fodder from my meadow began to recede faster than a mirage in front of a legless bedouin.

Soon after this I began waking up in the early hours, listening in dread for the swish of the milk van's tyres on the wet road. On with the wireless (I still won't call it a radio), and then the weather forecast. Then, having heard the worst, I would turn for reassurance to our local Air Force station where the friendly forecaster, such was the frequency of my telephone calls and so eager were my enquiries, must have been convinced that I was farming half Yorkshire. The needle of the barometer indicated the level of my spirits as accurately as it did the pressure of the air. The anxiety of it all resulted in my stomach, like the weather, becoming extremely unsettled.

Some eighteen years spent flying in the RAF had made me all too familiar with the scientific imprecision of weather forecasting in Britain. On one occasion I remember returning to base after a night flight to find half the airfield obliterated by fog. Whilst endeavouring to land on the other half I relayed this vital information to the met office, only to be told categorically that there could not be any fog since the air temperature was too high. The following morning I was informed by my Station Commander that, whatever the provocation, telling the met man to perform a physical impossibility with his thermometer, anemometer and any other meteorological instrumentation on which he could lay his hands was incorrect R/T procedure and must not be repeated.

The intervening years had not, it appeared, produced any notable improvements in the service. One morning, the words "Dry, sunny intervals and light winds" were almost drowned by the rattle of window panes and the Niagara-like roar of rain water gushing down from the roof. Such few fair weather periods as there were came entirely without warning and vanished almost before a surprised weather forecaster had time to jump into his sun suit.

At last there came a day when the monsoon let up long enough to allow the grass to be cut, a process that turned out to be a great deal more hazardous than expected. Hidden beneath the strands of Timothy, Meadow, Rye and Yorkshire Fog lay another crop — of stones. As the cutter laboured its way down the field it fought a rearguard action, firing high-speed missiles of varying sizes in a spray behind it, accompanied by the scream of tortured metal and the whizz and whirr of riccochetting pebbles. Hastily I beat a retreat to the nearest ditch, emerging only when, as often happened, the cutter had to stop for the blades to be repaired.

But, eventually, the job was complete and it goes without saying that, within hours, it was raining again. It rained almost without let-up for the next ten days, which I spent in agonies of indecision about when to turn or dash the now horizontal crop while various unused farm implements rusted in the field. It now appeared more than likely that, far from the crispy golden grass for which I had hoped, a few mouldy heaps of spinach-like texture were to be my lot. The depth of my depression at least equalled that of the one which was permanently centred over us, the troughs of which released their watery loads daily and sometimes nightly too.

It is nothing short of miraculous that there were eventually no less than 404 bales of good quality hay in my barn. This achievement, which provided enough fodder for that season and most of the next, also won me a number of side bets — wagers which, for the best part of a month, I had bitterly regretted entering into.

Not more than a day or so after the last bale had been pushed into place, I found myself sitting at a luncheon next to a landowner with rather larger interests than mine. The conversation, as so often happens between those with a love of the countryside and sport, touched on the weather and its effect on farming and sport. Before he had time to see the trap, I had launched into the dramatic history of my recent attempts at agriculture.

When his interest in my story seemed to be waning somewhat, I asked how much hay he was hoping to get in this year.

"About 70,000 bales," he replied. I turned quickly to my other neighbour and another subject before I could be forced to reveal the acreage of the modest meadow which had occupied my thoughts for so long.

IT'S THE AGE OF THE DRAIN

"A nice, full-bodied Wessex Saddleback . . . '69 I'd say.

I am now in a position to appreciate — and to sympathise with — Hercules' feelings, when first he surveyed 30 years' worth of accumulated deep litter left by 3000 oxen in the Augean stables. His ingenious solution to the problem was to divert the river Alpheus through the stables, thus saving himself many hours of blistering work with muck fork and wheelbarrow and possibly giving rise to the expression "flushed with success". In that respect, his task was much easier than mine. The nearest river is rather sluggish and nearly three miles away and, in any case, I doubt if Hercules would have had to worry about the local council's reaction to his water extraction scheme.

My problem is a ditch. Or, rather, what comes into it. The ditch itself lies across the middle of my field. Its contents appear from a large subterranean pipe on the boundary and pass under a small bridge before coming to rest in the ditch. When I bought the field, I was told that the ditch had a history and I could see for myself that it was by no means pure. Well, that is a bit of an understatement. On good days a patient observer can detect not so much a flow, more a sort of an ooze. On bad days it would take an expert glaciologist with some fairly sophisticated equipment to register any movement whatsoever and, long before he had time to record his findings, he would have passed out from the smell.

With what turned out to be a badly misplaced confidence in my ability to solve the problem, I completed the sale and set about constructing a letter to the appropriate Authority. Though I say it myself, that letter was a masterpiece. Pithy and succinct, it described, in a few well constructed sentences, the present intolerable situation and offered what I considered to be a reasonable and simple solution.

Exactly what effect my letter had on the Authority I do not know, for I have never had a reply to it. After a considerable lapse of time, feeling that my near-Herculean ingenuity deserved better, I resorted to the telephone, to discover that I should speak to the Pollution Officer, whose name was Pretty. "Have I got the name right?" I asked. Somehow the name Pretty and pollution did not seem to go together. But, yes, it was so.

In the interests of maintaining (dare I say?) the flow of this narrative, I will omit certain details of a repetitive nature at this point. Sufficient to say that, after a decent interval and a number of telephone calls, I received a personal visit. Together, Mr Pretty and I went and had a look and a sniff. Suitably impressed, on a subsequent visit he was pleased to accept a sample bottle of nicely matured Chateau Curtis, extracted with some difficulty from the point of entry.

The weeks passed and I began to worry that the entire staff of the Authority might have passed away, possibly overcome by fumes when they opened my gift sample. Could they have decided, I wondered, to let the matter drop? Or was it just going through the usual channels? Perhaps they had decided to wash their hands of the whole affair. Then, just when I had begun to despair, reinforcements arrived in the shape of the Parish Council.

To my surprise, I learned that my ditch was not the sole repository of nauseous effluent and that riparian owners farther down the line also had cause for complaint. Primed with this additional information a parochial broadside was fired at the Authority. Like the ditch, the plot was thickening.

At first I thought we had had another misfire but, after an interval of no more than a few weeks, I had another visitor. "My name's Rank," he said by way of introduction, "I've come about your ditch." Among the synonyms for the word 'rank' listed by Peter Roget are the following:

> *Fetid, strong-smelling, smelly, whiffy, malodorous, noisome, offensive, rancid, reasty, mouldy, fusty, musty, stuffy, frowsty, fuggy, foul, frowzy, olid, nidorous, stinking, rotten, putrescent, putrid, putrefying, tainted, high, mephitic, empyreumatic.*

Omitting one or two of the above, the exact meanings of which are not familiar to me, I had used nearly all these words to describe my ditch to the Authority, so the appearance of Mr Rank seemed fortuitous.

He proved, as I expected, to be a man of action. Without hesitation he stepped forward and dipped the toe of a Government issue wellington boot into the sludge-bound ditch. Then, bending down towards his upraised foot and inhaling deeply, with all the confidence of a wine connoisseur pronouncing on the product of a great vineyard, he said: "Pig!"

Realising that I was in the presence of a *real* authority, I modestly concurred with his opinion and went so far as to suggest its source. Together we followed the underground course up the hill, across the road and eventually to a line of drain covers pointing dramatically straight towards my suspect. At last we had arrived at the point of which I — and everyone else in the village — had been aware for years. It was at this point too, when I thought the battle all but won, that Mr Rank, while professing himself personally satisified as to the evil effluent's source, revealed that he was shortly to move to another post. The mopping up would be in the hands of another and, once again, I was left in the mire.

A lot more of what should have been water had passed under the bridge before I received another visit from the

Authority. Having asked tenderly after Mr Rank, I enquired, with some trepidation, the name of my latest visitor. "Beck," he replied.

And there the tale ends — well, not quite. Inspired by the information that the Authority believes the source of the offending ooze to have been traced and stopped, I have spent many an hour with a shovel in the ditch. Since neither Rome nor its sanitary arrangements were completed, so we are informed, within 24 hours, I am not expecting immediate results. But, nevertheless, I believe that Mr Beck will live up to his name and that, given time, the ominous belch of gaseous bubbles will one day give way to the cheerful tinkle of crystal clear water under the bridge.

P.S. Mr Beck did not live up to his name. I have now sold the field and the new owners are busy piping the drain. Good luck to them — and 'Cheers!'.

THE EWING FAMILY

I am lucky enough to have a wife. I'm sorry, I'll read that again. I am lucky enough to have a wife who owns a field from which my horse ingests enough fuel during the summer months to support me throughout the hunting season. Indeed, I am doubly blessed, for it is she who looks after said mount and prepares him, anything up to twice a week, for the chase. But, being the owner of the field, it is also she who has the final say about what shares the delectable thistles and other goodies that grow therein.

It is possible that an inherited trait has given my wife a penchant for sheep since, not only did her father farm woollies, but word has it that long dead ancestors once did naughty things around the border countries, like sequestering other people's flocks. Nowadays, probation or a spell of community service would doubtless be prescribed for such crimes, but for which the then penalty was terminal suspension from a gibbet. Whatever the cause, she has long hankered after a flock of her own and a chance conversation she had with someone I used to consider a friend led me to become familiar with the phrase 'rare breed' at the same time as she parted with a sizeable cheque.

Rare breeds have now become a sort of cult, complete with their own Society, and I in turn have become aware of *why* they became rare. The answer is simple; no one could catch them. 'Soay' is, I believe, an old Viking name for sheep in general and was the word used for calling one's sheep in days long past. Far up the map of Britain on the left hand side is an island called Soay in which a breed of small, horned sheep flourished and then (being uncatchable) diminished. I can only surmise that they leaped over the cliffs with some regularity. Certain it is that a cry of "Soay!" in our field, far from causing one to be surrounded by sheep, has about the same effect as does a loud "Tally Ho!" on a January fox.

From the foregoing you will have gathered (which, incidentally, actually, is more than I have ever been able to do with them) that we have bought a small flock of Soay sheep. They were injected into our field while we were away and, when we returned, barely visible above the grass were JR (the ram), Miss Ellie, Sue-Ellen and Pamela (the elder ladies) and Charlene and Lucy. The last five named were, we were assured, 'in lamb'.

Prior to their arrival we had erected, at vast expense, a supposedly impenetrable fence, capable (we hoped) of frustrating their reputed ability to vacate any enclosure in which they were put. Surprisingly, it worked — at least for a time. What we had not bargained with, however, was another reason why they are rare. Again, put simply, they don't do it. Well, ours hadn't. Long after the appointed time and during a freak blizzard there was a new arrival which, sadly, did not survive. Hourly from then on, having been assured that these things happen like clockwork, we attended the field. Hourly nothing happened until, having relaxed our guard, there was another. Since we dearly wanted ewe lambs in order to reduce the by now understandable rarity of the breed, it was, I suppose, inevitable that it should be the other sort. So was the next. And that was it.

So, with a flock vastly different in constitution from that

which we desired, we settled back to enjoy the summer and get to know them better. I had even built a shelter — we called it South Fork — but they refused to go inside, instead using the roof as a launching pad for attempts to go into orbit and it had to be demolished. Gradually they became tamer, so much so that JR actually fed from the hand and the others, while not venturing so close, at least came within viewing distance. Thus we were able to detect an infection in their eyes we discovered to be — and I promise you this is true — New Forest Disease. This, in a breed hailing from the wilds of West Scotland and which, we had been assured by that one-time friend to whom I referred earlier, were 'never any trouble at all'. While on the subject of that friend, I should perhaps mention that his daughter-in-law, on being informed whence came our sheep, dissolved into paroxysms of laughter, between spasms of which I was able to catch ". . . all over Norfolk . . . never in . . . neighbours always complaining . . . you didn't BUY them?" and such like.

To treat an eye infection, it is first necessary to apply some suitable medicament to the afflicted part and this, in turn, means having the patient within one's grasp. Whatever ideas you may have gleaned from watching 'One Man and his Dog', they will not, I assure you, apply to Soay sheep. Feed from your hand though they may, one's mere appearance in their field with thoughts of catching them will cause the fencing at the far end immediately to be put to the severest test. What is more, they can reduce a hitherto efficient dog to a shivering wreck in no time at all. One hears terrible tales of sheep-worrying by dogs. Our sheep are dog-worriers.

That we eventually caught them must be classified among the minor miracles of the twentieth century. The delay before we succeeded means that most of them now have far from perfect sight, a fact that renders them even harder to approach than before. They jump even higher when blind.

There are now three men and five women in the field, a status which looks like remaining reasonably quo, nature, I am reliably informed, dictating the time when things happen again. Before this occurs, the two juniors will have to be subtracted and then we will see if JR is really the chap we hope him to be. That time may not be too far away. With a strange gleam in his remaining eye, he charged me today. Providing he is not, so to speak, odd, we have every hope for next year.

In the meantime, should you be driving northwards up the A1 and chance to see a small flock of mixed brown and fawn coloured deer bounding down the southbound lane, there is a fair chance it's our lot returning to Norfolk.

Bull's-Eye View

When I'm led by the nose round the Shows there are those
Who think life on the farm is a ball;
That my purpose in life is to satisfy wife
After wife after wife — not at all!

Life was better by half as a little bull calf,
Motivated entirely by greed.
While Mum chewed the cud, a quick pull at her udder
Seemed to satisfy every last need.

Then, as I grew higher, so too my desire
For a heifer or two grew intense.
This met with frustration, my only sensation
Being a jolt from a volt in a fence.

When I wanted a cow (though my Dad told me how,
His methods are sadly outdated),
I was given the bird by the whole of the herd
Who'd been in (not by me) seminated.

It was fun being naughty with 30 or 40,
But now it's 1,000 or more
Life's not nearly so grand, for it's all done by hand
And, in fact, it's a terrible bore.

Here I stand in my pen only thinking of when
Things were **naturally** done and I sigh.
I'm a lonely old stud, slowly chewing the cud
As I wait for the man from A.I.

I'm a Champion Bull and my cup would be full
If they'd just let me out for a day
With a comely young cow and I would, here and now,
(Metaphorically speaking) make hay.

Drawings by Peggy Alexander

Pasture Pique

Nowadays we poor cows just produce milk and browse
And of calves have a regular issue.
Life's no longer so full since they cut out the bull
And — Oh Boy! — how we girls really miss you.

If we saw one of those with a ring in his nose,
Bovine hearts would be all of a flutter.
I'm a passionate cow and the sight of one now
Would churn all my pintas to butter.

Time was — come the spring — when we cows had a fling
With a lusty bull aristocrat.
It's a pretty dull life now I'm only the wife
Of a bull in a black bowler hat.

We're no longer called Daisy, or Mildred, or Maisie,
But a number that's stamped on one's back.
All our products are stored by the Marketing Board
And then served in a pasteurised pack.

No warm hands any more, no tin pails on the floor
Of the parlour, so sterile and clean;
No more kicking the stool and I feel such a fool
Being piped through a ruddy machine.

There is little to do but to chew and to moo,
As we stand there contentedly stolid.
In addition to that, there's the soft pit-a-pat,
Not of rain, but of something more solid.

So I'll munch round my field while increasing my yield
By ingesting a nourishing crop.
Then, to save myself strain, I'll digest it again —
Then I'll just let the whole matter drop.

Drawings by Peggy Alexander

EWE NEVER HAD IT SO GOOD

I'm a well-endowed ram and I've got where I am
By performing my act right on cue.
When it's time for a tup, I just line 'em all up
And shout "Volunteers? Ewe, ewe and ewe!"

ONE MAN AND HIS DOG

Sheepdog trials entail a rough ride in a trailer
For us sheep, then an up and down slog
Navigating round thistles, "Awaays", "Coom-bys" and whistles —
They should call it 'US sheep and THAT dog'.

SHEPHERD'S DELIGHT

When, at shows like the Royal, it gets hot, then I boil
For I'm wearing my coat, scarf and vest.
All the rest of my flock's had their annual defrock —
How I wish I had come here undressed!

KNIT-PICKING

As you sit at your loom, have you wondered from whom
Came the wool for your warp, woof or weft?
Yes, it's MY cloth you're wearing, sadly, after the shearing
Of my clothes there's nothing much left.

Drawings by Peggy Alexander

THE CLARION CROW

It is hard not to crow, when one's get up and go
Gets one up at a quarter past two.
So I wake up a hen and, until she says "When!",
I go cock, then I doodle and do.

EGGS-PRESS DELIVERY

Him up there, full of corn, wakes me up before dawn;
It's all strain until — look what I've done!
I'm completely eggshausted, I eventually forced it —
It's my very first egg — and size ONE!

THE LAYABOUT

Life's O.K., every day I just eat, cluck and lay,
Then I scratch as I range far and wide.
I can count myself lucky that I ain't in Kentucky,
For it's only my eggs that get fried.

WHICH CAME FIRST?

"Was I born?" "You were laid. It's when people are made,
They are born." *(The plot starts to thicken).*
"Mum, don't **people** get laid?" "Yes, they do I'm afraid,
Quite often — but not if they're chicken."

Drawings by Peggy Alexander

The Pig Tale

I'm a mobile rotunda with attachments down under —
Drinking places for piglets galore.
I am prone to inflation and give tit-elation
To dozens all squealing for more.

Who am I to deny it gets high in my sty?
And my life style you may not think well of;
I know that my belly is large and I'm smelly,
But it's **people** I can't stand the smell of.

Me, I like to think big, so I eat like a pig —
Of all food I'm an expert remover.
I prefer going hogging to press-ups or jogging,
Sucking scoff from my trough like a Hoover.

You see, God didn't mean us to be shapely like Venus;
He forgets to say "**WHEN**" when he pours,
But our men, for that matter, prefer us much fatter
And — thank goodness! — they're all crashing boars.

Drawings by Peggy Alexander

Across Country

TRIALS AND ERRORS

In the Services one is recruited for a job nobody wants by "I-want-three-volunteers-You-You-and-You." In civilian life it is done rather more subtly. First you hold a meeting at which, by accident or design, the "volunteer" you want is not present.

When the job that needs doing comes up for discussion everyone does their best not to catch the chairman's eye. Then the name of the absent one is mentioned. Immediately those who had sunk down in their chairs rise up with cries of "Jolly good chap, couldn't think of a better." "First-class idea." Feigned surprise "Oh, isn't he here?" Carried nem, as the Romans used to say, con.

I rode up to the Boxing Day meet with a fair sized hangover from the Christmas Day festivities. Separate tourniquets applied to each eye had prevented me from bleeding to death but various well known potions had entirely failed to dislodge a little man with a pneumatic drill who had taken up position athwart my right temple. One of my false teeth was aching quite badly.

At the risk of my head falling apart, I raised my hat to the Master and made a beeline for where the hair of the dog was being served up.

"Morning, Christopher, come and have a word with the Chairman for a moment." Dutifully I wheeled about.

On another day, in another place I might have escaped. As it was I had meekly run up the white flag in less than two minutes. The job of organising the Hunter Trials was mine.

The previous organiser was kind enough to give me some helpful advice on what was required. In no time at all, hazards of different shapes and sizes began to spring up — all of them equally fearsome. Perhaps the job wasn't so bad after all. At least not until I heard of the organiser's two "perks."

It was, apparently, a tradition that the organiser should be the first to attempt the horseborne circumnavigation of the course. To say that my hair turned white would be an exaggeration but there are, without doubt, numbers of grey hairs in my head which I swear were not there before receipt of this horrendous piece of news.

The other jolly perk that went with the job was emptying the elsans at the end of the day. Promises, promises. Empty ones, at that.

During the weeks preceding the day of the Trials, the thud of mallet on post, the tapping of nails, the occasional oath following the tapping of a thumb could be heard about the course. Flags, arrows and signs sprang up in bewildering profusion.

Darkness was falling on the evening before the great day when the final marker post went into the ground. Exhausted with my labours, I should have retired to bed at this point so as to be fresh for the horrors of the next day. However, in a foolish moment I was to regret, I had accepted an invitation to attend the annual Beagle Ball that evening and dinner with the Master before that. Worse still, it was the night for the clocks to go forward, which meant the loss of an hour's sleep.

The night was a good one, although I must confess that I am a little hazy about some of the details. For example, I can remember the port decanter coming round for the sixth (or was it the seventh?) time. On the other hand I am at a loss to explain my reasons for being on the outside of the banisters 15ft above the hall floor, though I have it on good authority that I indeed was.

People at the other end of the village have told me that they can clearly hear our alarm clock going off. That morning, in spite of the clock being about a foot away from my ear, I heard it not. The telephone ringing about an hour later did wake my wife, however — otherwise I doubt if I would have made the Trials at all. The reason for the telephone call was complicated. The wife of one of the previous night's party could not wake her husband and would I telephone to see if that would rouse him. I am glad to say it did.

It was thus that I arrived — just in time — on the course, leaving my wife to follow on with my horse. Which, I might add, she did, though not without incident, the trailer at one point becoming detached from the car and wedging itself in a gateway.

Ten o'clock. Time for the off! I clambered into the saddle, popped over a practice jump and rode up to the start. The Master pushed a large whisky into my hand and it went down without touching the sides. The white flag went down and I was away.

Not very far though. Horace didn't fancy the first fence and stopped. Cheers from the starting area. At the second attempt we made it. Sharp right and on to the next, a pole and ditch into the lane and out again over parallel bars. Rattle bang and something fell but we were out and away to the fourth.

The fourth was a stiffish hedge with a drop the other side. My drop came on the near side. At the second refusal Horace stopped a bit quicker than I did and I curved (quite gracefully, I am told) into the thorns. Undeterred by the sight of blood, I leaped aboard once more to collect a third refusal and elimination. At least I established a new course record with a fall, a knock down and four refusals without passing the fourth fence.

Next came the pairs. Now it so happened that my partner in the pairs was the very same person whose wife had been unable to wake him earlier. Moreover, his first round had, if anything, been more disastrous than mine. He had been eliminated at the first. The portents were not good and the portents were absolutely right.

Once again Andrew, my partner, stopped at the first though, surprisingly perhaps, I went over. I turned round to see him carry the fence away at the second attempt and then fall off. We were through! Pausing only for a quick pull at my flask, Andrew remounted and, to shouts of encouragement from a large crowd we charged at the in-and-out over the lane. Up and over. Apart from clanging together in mid-air these obstacles were surmounted successfully but, once again, the fourth was — literally — my downfall.

Three refusals each and a fall by me led to a quick conference as to our future progress. It resulted in a decision to miss out 4, 5 and 6 and we came in at the seventh. Over the parallel bars, down the drop wall, beautifully together over the pheasant coops and then a nicely matched refusal at the tenth.

So we missed out that one and the next, jumped out of the lane, in fine style over the open ditch and thence to the tiger trap. Here, still going well, we appeared once again in view of the by now highly puzzled spectators, the commentator having announced we were eliminated at least twice. To a chorus of hunting horns, holloas and cheers, we swept past down the hill over the burn, jumped the last three and eventually galloped through the finishing line.

What with the falls, a fairly steady intake of restoratives and all the other excitements of the day, the other duty I had to perform quite slipped my mind. I remembered the elsans three days later.

TEAM SPIRIT

"I SAY — 'Are you ready?' ONCE — ARE you ready? — ROW!" The last time I heard that command it issued from a portly, white-flannelled figure who overflowed a most inadequate looking bicycle and atop whose head was perched a pink Leander cap, producing an effect of a mobile, pear-shaped, cream-covered blancmange with strawberry topping. It is not, however, that mental picture which haunts me, rather it is the dreadful sense of foreboding which always filled the moments immediately prior to taking the first stroke. A nightmarish certainty would grow that, whatever the other seven oarsmen were going to do, muggins would either be left immobile or, even worse, catch an enormous crab.

I have heard it said, by one with experience in both fields, that the dread he experienced just before a big rowing race was only equalled by that he felt when lined up for the start of the Grand National. Be that as it may, it was not until I found myself a member of a team ready for the 'off' in a cross-country event that the old familiar feeling hit me once again. I use the expression "found myself a member of a team" advisedly, since no one in their right mind would select me unless, as happened in this case, they were unable to find anyone else.

True, I had taken part, with varying degrees of failure, in a number of hunter trials, but such well justified premonitions as I had had on these occasions were as nothing compared with the doom-laden thoughts with which I approached the starting line with the rest of the team. The first time I had gone solo, I was too ignorant to know what might be in store and the Master's generous offer of a large whisky, quickly accepted, helped allay any qualms. After that performance, which terminated with my retirement in the depths of a thorn hedge comprising the fourth fence, things could only improve — and did, only marginally though, as I have already related.

The first stages of being a team member are fine. "We're only going for the fun of it, of course," "Just a bit of a jolly, really," and other remarks designed to imbue the unwilling recruit with confidence are bandied about. Then, gradually, things become more serious. "I see the prizes go down to number six — we might have a chance" starts an icy shiver running down my spine. This is followed by the information that, since there is a prize for the best turned out team, we must perform in full fig. The sight of a top hat, sailing in solitary splendour over the first fence, whatever it may provide in the way of entertainment for the spectators, does absolutely nothing for the self-esteem of its owner. The light-hearted atmosphere of yesterday has already evaporated.

Come viewing day and the situation deteriorates even further. Sheer professionalism takes over as the, to me, bewildering complexities of jumping each obstacle are discussed at length. The number of strides between A and B, a matter I have always left entirely to my horse, are worked out in detail. By the time we reach the sixth fence I am devising a number of ways by which I can withdraw without too much loss of face. "We'll pop this one," says one. Pop? I am more than likely to expire with a loud bang over that one.

Barely able to see over the top of a fearsome hedge from the drop side, I observe that it is preceded by a yawning ditch and sneak off to have a look at its lesser alternative. Faced with an imposing set of unbreakable (and, to my mind, insurmountable) rails, I am informed that it will jump perfectly. Before I have time to mention that it is ME that is meant to do the jumping, I am told that "This is a jolly good course for horses." Indeed? That, surely, is not the point. I am well aware that my horse is fully capable of going round the course. There is little point in his achieving this feat, however, unless I accompany him — an eventuality of which there seems less and less likelihood with every new fence we inspect.

By now, I feel like a condemned pirate, forced to inspect the plank along which he will shortly be made to walk. In spite of my better feelings and my loudly expressed doubts, I am persuaded to remain a member of the team. Even a carefully rehearsed limp and the discovery of a number of previously unmentioned ailments are not allowed to excuse me from what has now become a duty to perform.

A marked increase in the consumption of cigarettes and some sleepless nights mark the passage of time between viewing and actuality until, all too swiftly, the day comes. Urgent preparations leave little time for thought. It is not until, mounted and in the collecting ring that I am seized with the old terror. The butterflies in my tummy loop the loop before dropping dead in an inert mass as I observe a mud-bespattered competitor leading a limping horse back from some disaster on the course.

Then, suddenly, our team is called. My final cigarette tumbles from between shaking fingers, rather, I imagine, as it must from the hand of a man attached to a stake just before the blindfold is put on. All thoughts of our carefully laid plan as to how we were to approach the first fence forgotten, we reach the starting line, only to discover that the previous team has demolished a fence and that there will be a delay. The whole team's nerves are now in shreds but, just before we actually come to blows or one of the horses has time to lash out, the white flag drops, we're off and, much to my surprise, I find myself safely over the first fence.

Details of the next few minutes remain a trifle hazy, my next clear recollection being of passing the finishing line, miraculously still united with my horse. Our event is sponsored by Theakstons, the Masham brewers, and is rightly renowned for the amount of liquid hospitality dispensed during the day. Team spirit was flowing in large quantities when I reached the bar and it was not long before I found myself saying I wouldn't mind going again the next year. Of course, there is always the problem of finding a team that will accept me as a member.

MORE Team Spirit

Team Chasing's a sport I, for one, find so fraught
That it scares me right out of my wits.
Every time I set out, in my mind there's no doubt
I'll return (if at all) in small bits.

It's too late to say "No," for I've said I will go
And of course I can't let down the side.
But I'm ruing the day that I heard myself say,
"Yes, I'll just come along for the ride."

As we walk round the course — how much worse on a horse! —
I'm appalled by the height of each fence
And, as they get higher so, too, my desire
To take a quick trip to the gents.

On the day of the Chase, I confess that the pace
Of my pulse is a hundred and four,
But it feels less frisky after two gulps of whisky;
It's quite calm after several more.

We are all well alight and my horse, taking fright,
Lashes out and I hear myself cursed.
The flag drops — we've started! I find myself carted
At a furious speed to the first.

I am minus my hat when I've got over that,
But kick on! Through some rails with a crash,
Turn left after seven, three more to eleven;
It's the water — whoa! — steady there! — SPLASH!

We were going quite well until Philippa fell
And two of us crashed in mid-air.
Reg's horse had a stop on one side of the drop,
Though he's over with plenty to spare.

The next's a big hedge, Jan clears it then Reg,
Remounted, and I arrive puffing.
Although we survive it, I think we deprive it
Of most of its poles and its stuffing.

Downhill to the last, we are all going fast;
Up and over! We scatter the crowd.
My goodness, we've done it! Though, alas, we've not won it
Being over the time that's allowed.

It all seems such fun when it's over and done
And team spirit's poured out in huge measures.
I say, "Let's go again!" For the grief and the pain
Are forgotten among all the pleasures.

When the spirit has died — and my longing to ride —
I regret what I said when in wine.
If you're after a place in another Team Chase,
Let me know — you are welcome to mine!

Drawings by John Tickner

BOOT-TO-BOOT

JET

Stamina, boldness and strong legs — these are the qualities I look for in a good point-to-pointer. Other attributes I like to see are the ability to avoid getting bunched at the start and to cope with any type of going, as well as a good strong head. As to the horses . . .

Yes, it is the *racegoers*, as opposed to the *runners*, to whom I refer and, for newcomers to the sport of point-to-pointing, I hope that the following advice may help them to avoid some of the many pitfalls which may mar their enjoyment of what can be a very entertaining day.

For a start, the title 'Point-to-Point' may give the impression that you have a choice of places at which to stand, depending on whether you wish to see the start or the finish. This is not so, the races being run nowadays on a more or less circular basis. Not that spectating is necessarily the main aim of many who attend such meetings — far from it. There are those to whom the races come only as brief interruptions in a day of almost continuous self-indulgence, as they move from the rear end of one well-stocked car to another. For them, a more appropriate title might be 'Boot-to-Boot'.*

Though many courses have now reached a standard

* If you are American, this should read 'Trunk-to-Trunk'.

little short of the established race tracks, the majority have retained a subtle charm and a special atmosphere which modernisation may have dented but not destroyed. Unlike the popular race meetings, the crowd at point-to-points is usually about right — small enough to meet all one's friends, but also of a size sufficient to avoid those to whom one does not want to speak. Then again, there is room for the children to disappear without them becoming hopelessly lost and the subsequent need for embarrassing loudspeaker announcements.

First, however, there is the need to avoid a false start. The approaches to a point-to-point are, more often than not, extremely rustic, consisting of a farm track which, though perfectly capable of coping with the passage of the occasional tractor, is liable to subside under the onslaught of several hundred cars.

Should the day prove unexpectedly fine, an unexpectedly large number of cars will form a huge queue, the drivers all apparently eager to test their springs out on the deeply rutted track. Those arriving with the intention of seeing the first race will be lucky to see the second. In the event of less clement weather, a queue will still form. This will be caused by the inevitable driver who does not appreciate that heavy use of the accelerator in muddy conditions does not propel a car forwards, but downwards. Any shouted advice will be drowned in the tortured roar of the engine and those who attempt physical aid will be drowned in the fine spray of liquid ooze ejected by the madly spinning wheels.

If you have managed to beat the queue by arriving early, your first hazard will be a number of retainers, the first of whom will extract from you a sum of money for the privilege of being allowed to wreck your car's suspension. You will be relieved to know that you are allowed a second go for free, on the way out. That is, of course, provided you do not need the services of a tractor, in which case your return trip will prove even more expensive. Experienced hands, having paid their dues to the man on the gate, will then ignore the frantic gestures of those appointed to park the cars in neat rows. Instead, they will park at some spot from which they know they can easily make a getaway at the end of the day.

Careful planning is just as necessary to make the best possible use of the time available and thus obtain the maximum enjoyment from the day's racing. The usual card allows 35 minutes between races, but this may be shortened if, as sometimes happens, the first race is late in starting. Say half-an-hour then, of which the race itself will take up some ten minutes. During the remaining 20 minutes there is a variety of activities which may be carried out:

1. Looking at the runners in the paddock (at the riders too in the ladies' race).
2. Marking one's card.
3. Picking up a good tip.
4. Studying the bookies' odds.
5. Queueing at the Tote.
6. Having a drink.
7. Talking to friends (if any).
8. Positioning oneself at a good vantage point for the race.

Candidates intending to attempt all eight will deduce by a simple mathematical calculation that there are only 2½ minutes available for each activity — even less if other equally important diversions are to be included. Looking for one's wife, for example. Looking for someone else's, for another. There may also be the exercising of dogs, the searching for children, or even a visit to what are laughingly described as the facilities. These latter can, with the aid of a pair of field glasses, sometimes be recognised by a sign saying SⱢNƎƆ hanging on a piece of sacking about three-quarters of a mile away. If you make the distance, you will know you are in one of the posher ones by the fact that a divot has been removed to indicate the intended direction of flow. As for the Ladies — I am advised that they should not.

You will have realised by now that it may be necessary to combine two or more of activities 1 - 8 in order to achieve par for the course. An example of how this can be achieved might be "How-nice-to-see-you-both-thanks-I'll-have-a-whisky-how-do-you-do-how-do-you-do-what's-going-to-win-the-next?-thank-you-goodbye," but such an approach may lose one a useful source of information unless carried out with the maximum tact, although it will have disposed of three items in under a minute. Care should also be taken over the frequency with which activity No. 6 is attempted, lest the consequent necessity to visit the SLNEƆ further reduces the time available.

I hope I have shown that a visit to a Point-to-Point Meeting should not be undertaken without a considerable amount of forethought and pre-planning. The effort involved will be well rewarded by an enjoyable day at one of the great country sports.

Oh, I almost forgot. Don't forget to leave time to collect your winnings — if any.

Boot-to-Boot (another step)

Those who like to go up for the Ascot Gold Cup,
Or to Aintree, the Derby or Oaks
Wear their smart suits and hats, I can tell you that that's
Not the gear for US race-going folks.

We abandon our tellies and we pull on our wellies
To go off to our Point-to-Point Meeting.
Why not give it a go, you'll enjoy it, I know —
An occasion that takes all the beating.

First, avoid being late, getting stuck in a gate
Behind an old banger, wheels spinning,
Which throws mud over you and the rest of the queue
While your tip for the first race is winning.

You can go for the thrills, for the jumping and spills,
Or in hope of not backing a loser;
Quite a few who go there, as they say, for the beer
Spend the whole of the day in the boozer.

Others, out for a toot, simply go boot-to-boot,
Barely seeing each race as it passes,
Indulging their pleasures in very large measures —
Not through field, but in spirit-sized glasses.

Keep your drinks fairly short, or it's short you'll get caught
(And a very long walk, all uphill it is)
For those two distant tents, one marked LADIES one GENTS
Are what's laughably termed 'the facilities'.

Our friends are complacent they'll win the Adjacent,
So we back it each way for a pound.
But it's form reads O-PUFF (and it's right) sure enough
Out of puff it has run half way round.

It's the Ladies Race next and a question that's vexed
Many punters in need of a tip.
Will the prettiest eyes, or the sturdiest thighs,
Or the girl with the form get the trip?

In the Members old Jack is the one NOT to back,
There he goes, up and over — oh dear!
They've just gone to fetch a bone-setter and stretcher
For the fourteenth consecutive year.

When they've run the last race, keep some money in case
You get stuck or your car will not go.
For I'm willing to bet, you'll be sitting there yet
If you can't ante up for a tow.

Drawings by John Tickner

DOWNHILL ALL THE WAY

Those who know me will appreciate that this tale is about going downhill in the gravitational and not the moral sense, an abstemious life or self-denial having always been my aim.

One of my earliest memories is of the brief flight I made, headfirst, from first floor bannister rail to ground floor stone and, later, there was the downhill journey I made in an open car which would have been unremarkable had the car not been inverted at the time. Since half the world's population are stiff with back problems and the other half bored stiff listening to their complaints, I will not elaborate on the combination of events which put me in hospital, plaster and eventually under the surgeon. Sufficient to say that the above, plus a number of other incidents have convinced me that Newton definitely had something; furthermore, if the state of my body is anything to go by, the apple which inspired him must have been uneatable.

Paradoxical it is, then, that I have always had a yen to go downhill in one of the fastest possible ways — on a toboggan. This (dare I say?) inclination stems from the time I spent sharing a room during flying training with someone who became a legend in the art of headfirst descent down the Cresta. Unable to sample the sport then, years passed without another opportunity until, more than three decades later, I chanced to meet someone who himself had been down the slippery slope and I was foolish enough to reveal the longing I had always had.

At the time of this revelation I was standing in a meadow a few miles distant from Inverness, a safe enough place, one would have thought, to publicise one's inner-most desires. Not a bit of it. A large hand descended with some force on my shoulder and, recovering from this unwarranted attack, I turned to find a tall, kilted figure assuring me that I was welcome to stay in his flat in St Moritz and sample the heady delights of tobogganing. Like most things that have got me into trouble, it seemed a jolly good idea at the time.

I used to do a lot of sailing in my younger days and it was, I believe, HRH The Duke of Edinburgh who likened that sport to standing under a shower and tearing up £10 notes (with inflation, probably £50 notes by now). By the same token, tobogganing down the Cresta could be likened to renting a very expensive penthouse suite and spending the week throwing oneself headfirst from the balcony. But, before I take you down the precipitous slide, I should explain that I accepted the invitation in high summer and several months and most of a hunting season were to pass before my nerve was to be put to the ultimate test. Indeed, my well known ability in the art of unplanned descents from horses made it probable that I would not be fit to go when the time came. Nor, almost, was I.

By some miracle, the season in question passed virtually without incident, that is until the very last day's hunting before I was due to head for Switzerland. The first fence of the day was stiffish — parallel rails either side of an embryo hedge — and Shamus' sudden realisation that the second rail had to be jumped at the same time as the first caused him to come to an abrupt halt, depositing me neatly between the two. With nothing worse than bruised pride, I set about remounting. Now Shamus is, as befits a horse that has to carry me, quite large and, with his dander up early in the hunt, extremely hard to climb aboard, so this operation took some time. Long enough, in fact, for the hunt to be decimated at the next fence due to a hidden strand of wire in the top of the hedge.

By the time I had remounted and safely negotiated the first hazard, the disaster area had been cleared and all I could see was an inviting hedge before me and, beyond that, the hunt well on. We therefore approached at considerable speed. There was no warning of disaster, just a loud twang, not dissimilar to the sound of a belly dancer's g-string I once heard snap in a Turkish night club, and we came to an abrupt stop in mid-air. The effect of Shamus' feet connecting with the wire caused every-thing to halt except my teeth, which left my mouth at some speed. It also caused Shamus and, perforce, me too to rotate. On my way down I was quick (and stupid) enough to catch my teeth just as they hit the ground and everything after that is a bit hazy. Whether my hat was still on my head when I landed, or whether Shamus rolled on it after he rolled on me, I do not know. In any event, its shape caused me to consider returning it to the makers in a large envelope. My own state was scarcely any better.

It was my teeth that did the damage as they, or rather their predecessors, had done on another occasion many years before. Then, in my bachelor days, it was my wont to leave my teeth overnight in a glass or bowl and, returning late from a very good party, I carelessly shied them into the basin before retiring. The inaccuracy of my aim only became apparent when, having overslept and leaping quickly out of bed, I was impaled on my dentures and thereby became possibly the only person in the world to need the services of a doctor after biting himself on the foot. On this occasion it was my hand, later found to have a broken bone, which suffered and this, together with a number of painful bruises, made the journey to St Moritz by train, aircraft and car, a fairly uncomfortable one.

After a hair-raising last few miles in heavy snow, we arrived at our destination around midnight to find the flat locked and deserted. However, our disappointment was turned to joy when, driving round the town, we heard the sound of bagpipes percolating through the steamed-up windows of a restaurant. Within, there was my host puffing away, accompanied by another piper whom I also knew. Being celebrated were the Inter-Services Cresta Championships and I had no trouble in collecting a headache in addition to my other aches and pains by the time it came to line up for my first bash at the Cresta.

The Cresta, by the way, is the one you descend by yourself, lying prone on a heavy metal toboggan. The course is solid ice, very narrow, with sheer sides and a number of corners, the most notorious of which, Shuttle-cock, has no top to the bank. The purpose of this is to allow people like myself to become members of the Shuttlecock Club, the sole qualification for which is to go too fast round it and zoom spectacularly off the course. The distance from Junction to finish is about half a mile with a drop of some 330 feet. Riders are provided with an assortment of protective clothing, crash helmet, goggles, metal-backed gloves, elbow and knee pads and boots with steel-toothed toecaps. However, the hoped for anonimity provided by this disguise is removed by the announcement of one's name as the next to go.

It is at this point that the terror sets in and a strong

desire to ask permission to leave the room comes upon one. The first start is a rather undignified affair, the prone position being adopted while the toboggan is restrained by the starter's foot. The agony of what seems an interminable wait in this position is added to by the horrible thought that fear may cause one to disgrace oneself and the ribald comments of one's watching friends who tell you that you already have. A bell rings, the foot is removed and, in spite of raking hard with one's toecaps as

C.C.

instructed, the acceleration is fearsome. Faster and faster, banging from side to side of the track, up one bank, down and up another. Under the bridges, a last sharp drop and suddenly it's over. All is silence apart from the sound of me taking my first breath for a minute. The extraordinary thing is that my one thought at that moment was to get back up the hill and do it again, only better.

Subsequent starts are made with a run and a flying leap onto the toboggan and times, apart from the three occasions on which the clock stopped at Shuttlecock, steadily improved. The week flew by in a welter of parties and early starts, for the run closes at midday when the sun is beginning to melt it. All too soon I heard over the loudspeaker the final "Terminato", the traditional announcement of the run's closure for the day.

While I had been away, there had been no hunting, due to frost. It thawed the day I returned and, thanks to my wife, I was able to step out of the train and onto my horse for a perfectly splendid day's hunting, without so much as a single fall.

> A bass tenor who rode *moderato*,
> Lost control and went much too *staccato*.
> His toboggan (*vibrato*)
> Flipped and now he's *castrato* —
> His career, sad to say, *'Terminato'*.

While happy to say that I am in better shape than the unfortunate singer, it is time, nevertheless, for me also to say *'Terminato'*.

They're Off!

When I go to the Races — flat, hurdle, or 'chases,
There is plenty of help and advice
On which horses to back and, though there's no lack,
It doesn't come cheap at the price.

The man on the gate says, "Back number eight
In the first, for I swear it can't fail."
But it's money ill-spent, for the pace that it went
Was that of an elderly snail.

When it came to the second, a trainer friend reckoned,
"My hurdler, it cannot be beat."
He might have been right if, at the last flight,
It had managed to stay on its feet.

From an owner I heard that his horse in the third
Was just right and was bound to go close.
But his horse was deformed and he'd been misinformed,
Unless someone had slipped it a dose.

Then a jockey I know said, "This one will go.
It will win — get your money on fast."
Going better than most, it was first past the post
But its rider, on foot, finished last.

And then I met Nancy who told me her fancy
Had scored with a ten-to-one win.
My choice wasn't there and it's no help to hear
She chose hers with the help of a pin.

My next choice was good, for it gamely withstood
Every challenge and went fit to bust.
But, alas, it was pipped and, thoroughly gypped,
I tore up my slips in disgust.

And then an objection advanced my selection
To first. But to my dismay,
Though I searched all the ground in the bar and around,
Every piece had been blown away.

And that's why you see foolish fellows like me,
Who put money on other men's choices,
Walking round without shirts (which we've lost on dead certs)
While bookies drive round in Rolls Royces.

Drawings by John Tickner

Leaping to Conclusions

From being born by a bog, it's an arduous slog
To becoming a show horse or hunter;
Harder still for us horses who are leaping round courses,
Bringing joy to the bookie or punter.

Oh, how slowly days pass, when I'm turned out to grass,
While my other end swishes at flies.
I'm denied any fun by a cut that was done
In my youth — and brought tears to my eyes.

Once arrived at a yard, life begins to get hard,
Though the food, on the whole, isn't bad;
For I'm forced to maintain a routine by my trainer
And a man (or a girl) called a lad.

How frenetic the pace is when preparing for races,
Then a long, dreary ride in the box.
How I envy my friends, paying no dividends
And who jump in pursuit of the fox.

Here we go, once again, on the old gravy train,
Around paddocks which all look the same.
Wait a moment — this crowd! And the shouting's so loud;
It's the Festival — Cheltenham — Fame!

Hoi polloi, Dukes and Queens are all packed like sardines
Into boxes and stands and the terraces;
As I join the parade, final bets are being laid
And the tipsters still whispering heresies.

Going down to the start, I begin to take heart,
For this circuit is better than most.
It's not fences I mind, but that long, uphill grind
From the last to the finishing post.

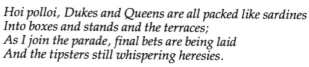

Him on top sticks my nose in a fence, I suppose
That he thinks I don't know what I'm here for.
Then, around we go paddling, because someone's resaddling —
Not a ploy that the rest of us care for.

"Make a line!" Up we trot and "THEY'RE OFF!" — no we're not,
As a last minute turner gets cursed.
At the second attempt, no one tries to pre-empt
And away we all go to the first.

Some you win, some you lose — when one wins, Owners booze,
I get neck-aching, rump-stinging slaps.
If I'm not even placed, I return home disgraced;
My fault — or the jockey's, perhaps?

Since my new syndication, end-of-race celebration
In the winner's enclosure is hell.
For I now have **four** owners and — an unwanted bonus —
All their wives want to slap me as well.

Drawings by John Tickner

Cartwheels Across Country

4 WHEELS ON MY WAGON
Section E and we're ready to go.
We caused a sensation
With our slick Presentation,
Now we're off! — the first hazard — we're . . . OH!

3 WHEELS ON MY WAGON
Now the strain is beginning to show.
First, a judge gets a nudge,
Then a post doesn't budge —
Oops! Another one's gone from below.

2 WHEELS ON MY WAGON
And the pace is beginning to slow.
We come out of the water
Yet another wheel shorter —
Sacré bleu! Ah, mon Dieu! Pauvres chevaux!

1 WHEEL ON MY WAGON
And the horses are starting to blow.
Round a corner we skid,
But at least it gets rid
Of the last (which was somewhat *de trop*).

NO WHEELS ON BY WAGON
And we are, you might say, a bit low.
But we're nearing the end
And, around the next bend
Is the Finish. Disqualified??? NO!

4 WHEELS BACK ON MY WAGON
Adrenalin's starting to flow.
But my gallant groom feels
That, to keep all our wheels,
My vocabulary **must** include WHOA!

Drawings by John Tickner

Caveat Emptor

(let the buyer beware)

Young man if, perforce, you must purchase a horse,
Then of dealers like Paddy beware.
Of people whose words from the trees can charm birds
Or the cash from your wallet — take care!

I went to his farm and I fell for his charm
When he showed me his 'wonderful horse'.
With his rich Irish brogue this most plausible rogue
Took me in — and I bought it, of course.

"I don't like to brag, but he jumps like a stag
Over timber and hedges and water.
I am sure he will do as a hunter for you
And gentle enough for your daughter.

"D'ye want him for racing? He's bred right for 'chasing,
Both his dam and his sire won a lot.
He has a full brother — belongs to me mother —
Who won ten point-to-points on the trot.

"He's as safe in a box as the gold in Fort Knox
And he goes like a bomb with the hounds.
He is easy to clip. He's an absolute snip
At a thousand — that's guineas not pounds.

"A child could be doing this grooming and shoeing,
In the ring you should see his clear rounds.
He's a horse you will bless, so I couldn't take less
Than nine hundred. Come now, I'll take pounds.

"He's only just eight and well up to the weight
And at dressage he really astounds.
He's a real good goer, I couldn't go lower
Than eight hundred. For cash I'll take pounds.

"At showing he's grand. Just you look at him stand,
In good points you can see he abounds.
Ah sure, sir, as buyer you will have to go higher
Than five hundred and twenty-five pounds.

"He always goes well and as sound as a bell.
What? You think that this looks like a spavin?
Ah no. Not at all — just a little wind gall —
'Tis a wonderful horse you'll be havin'.

"All right, I'll say seven. As God's in His heaven,
You can have him at that price because
You're the man for the horse. Sir, your gain is my loss."
So at last I said: "DONE" — and I was.

And that is the reason I lost a whole season
As well as a few hundred smackers.
And I'm filled with remorse that the worth of that horse
Was eighteen pounds ten at the knackers.

Take warning, my son, or you too will be done
If you don't see the point of this tale.
Beware of the blarney of Paddy O'Mahoney
And of others with horses for sale.

Illustrated by John Tickner

Mixed Bag

INTO THE VALLEY OF DEATH . . .

J.E.T.

The invitation to take part in a film generated immediate visions of my name up in lights. I could see it all. It would be like one of those epics in which the sadly late John Wayne, as a cavalry officer, sword outstretched, gallops unscathed through a hail of bullets while the villains, well ventilated by forty-fives, fall in disorderly heaps like so many discarded cullenders.

True, my deportment and standard of horsemanship may not be of a quality to inspire others to follow me into the jaws of death, nor, it must be admitted, was Horace's breeding of the sort to make him an obvious choice to play a Champion the Wonder Horse part. No matter, the chance of instant stardom could not be lightly dismissed.

Adroit camera work and expert directorship would doubtless combine to eliminate any evidence of miscasting and we would emerge in a suitably heroic portrayal to leave audiences gasping on the edge of their seats at our dare-devil exploits. Could there, I wondered, be a scene in which, with Horace's help, I rescued a damsel in distress? No, that would be asking too much in this our first starring role, and anyway Horace's back legs probably wouldn't stand up to a double load.

"Yes," I replied, "Horace and I would be delighted to take part in a film."

It had all started when our Master, during a chance visit to a local hostelry, was accosted by a gentleman who asked whether he was, as he had been given to understand, Master of the local pack of hounds. Since the gentleman's appearance was not such as to inspire any confidence that he could be even remotely interested in next season's sporting prospects, the Master's reply was somewhat non-committal.

Eventually it transpired that the inquirer was a film producer desirous of a number of first world war cavalry officers, complete with horses, to appear in a scene which was to be filmed in the market town lying almost in the centre of our hunt country. It would all be done in one day and, yes, there would be suitable remuneration. This last consideration was the deciding factor and the deal was speedily concluded over a glass or two.

With hindsight I can see that I was not, perhaps, an immediate choice, but the request came at a time, during the close season, when not everyone can instantly produce a suitable mount. However, such thoughts did not cloud my mental horizon when the clarion call of duty rang out. Came the appointed day and I reported (at an unearthly hour for a Sunday morning) to the Town Hall, where a large proportion of Yorkshire's population had also fore-gathered to be made up and dressed in the appropriate period costumes and uniforms.

We emerged, an hour or so later, covered in embarrassment as well as make-up, attired in a weird mixture of ill-fitting uniforms and with our faces for the most part hidden by long, droopy moustaches. Our discomfiture was in no way reduced by the howls of mirth which greeted our appearance from an assortment of friends and relations who had gathered to see the fun. Horace failed to recognise me and shied like a startled mustang when I attempted to mount.

The scene in which we were to take part involved the visit of an official deputation to the town in order to recruit volunteers for the British Expeditionary Force in France. The procession included a Government Minister, the Mayor, and other local dignitaries and, of course, a military band with its escort of cavalry officers mounted on their chargers.

The Master, no doubt fancying himself in the star part, had annexed the place of honour at the head of this motley mob and Horace and I found ourselves relegated to a position immediately to the rear of the band. It required no great stretch of the imagination to appreciate that Horace and I, far from filling the wide screen, would be lucky to appear as anything better than a barely distinguishable blur, occasionally bobbing into sight from behind the big drum. Ah, well, over-night stardom has, I believe, sprung from lesser beginnings.

There was a lot of shuffling about while men with wireless sets and megaphones dashed about. Positioned as we were at the tail-end, the order to advance did not reach us. The first intimation we had that things were under way was a sudden and discordant cacophony of sound emanating from the instrumentalists in front of us. Horace (and who can blame him?) took exception to the manner in which he was awakened from the slumber into which he had fallen and took off into a nearby flowerbed. Only with the greatest difficulty did I remain in the saddle.

An inauspicious start, but worse was to come. As we entered the main street, the well-briefed local residents erupted from their houses, waving and cheering while what seemed like thousands of small children, equipped with Union Jacks, whistles and rattles, ran alongside us adding to the already deafening din. To this, also, Horace demurred, particularly when an ill-mannered urchin applied the point of a flagstick to his not-inconsiderable rear end.

114

This was just a practice run. At the end of the street we executed an about-turn and returned to our starting place. Again the clash of cymbals and the advance was repeated. By now the wretched ragamuffin with the pointed stick, possibly on the orders of a malicious film director, had decided that a more or less regular posterial prod was to be a feature of the film. This time, however, Horace got his own back, releasing a large quantity of well-digested food on to the roadway in front of the offensive child, who was, I am glad to say, barefoot. Thereafter we were able to proceed unmolested.

Far from that being the final run, it was only the second of many that took us back and forth up and down the street until well past lunchtime. When the time for a break finally came, the cavalry fell in in double-quick order at the bar of the nearest inn where, eschewing the more solid refreshment on offer and pausing only to elevate our moustaches enough to allow the application of a glass, we became what might be described as reasonably well oiled.

The afternoon saw a repeat performance of the morning's activities, the procession parading interminably through different parts of the town. The effects of the liquid luncheon and a steaming hot day began to tell. Make-up ran in rivulets down weary faces and once proud moustachios slid grotesquely down tired chins. The horses, by now inured to anything, were one and all asleep, waking only to snatch a chance carrot from one of the many market stalls.

At one point an eager sound-effects man ran beside me, his boom microphone held close to Horace's feet to record the clip-clop of British cavalry on the move. I had not the heart to tell him that, of all the horses on parade, Horace was the only one without any shoes — our blacksmith being on holiday at the time. He must have been mystified, when playing it over that night, to hear, instead of the expected clatter, a gentle phut-phutting sound.

The evening session saw us all assembled in the market square for the "Your country needs you" speeches by the aforementioned dignitaries. To our great relief, lined up behind a raised dias, we discovered that my wife and a large basket containing alcoholic refreshment could remain concealed from the cameras behind a huge Union

Jack which draped the platform. From this advantageous position she dashed out between scenes with liquid nourishment. Sort of shots between shots, so to speak.

Even so, the day was long and wearisome and it ended with a lengthy haggle over the monetary value of our contribution to the proceedings. The final agreement resulted in Horace being paid exactly twice as much as I was. In spite of the disappointment caused by my realisation that a star would not, at least for the time being, adorn my dressing-room door, I think he deserved every penny of it.

Taking the Pith out of Polo

In the days of the Raj and the cavalry charge,
Men and helmets were all full of pith.
Things aren't nearly so pukka, now the place for a chukka
Is the lawn of some fellow called Smith.

Drawings by John Tickner

An Eventful Day

While you're driving back home from our local event,
Perhaps you'll be saying, "How well it all went!"
But you'd say something else if, like me, you had spent
From dawn until dusk in the Secretary's Tent.

The ground's in its usual terrible state
And the very first horsebox gets stuck in the gate;
At last, here's the Doctor, but where is the Vet?
And one of the Fence Judges isn't here yet;
That silly young girl has forgotten to bring
The watches we need for the show-jumping ring;
If I'm any judge of this Judge's demeanour,
He's late and he can't find the dressage arena;
The barman's complaining he can't find the booze;
There's another complaint on the state of the loos;
The fence mender's wanted at three different fences;
The man in the car park's demanding expenses;
The water jump's causing a great deal of grief
And it's time for the fence judge to have a relief;
The man on the commentary hiccoughs and swears
With the microphone on — and so everyone hears;
A parent's insisting we've got the wrong score
And behind her are bound to be quite a few more;
A very small child, a pink purse and some keys
Have been found (one in tears), "Will the owners come, please."
Excitement is rising, we are quite near the end,
Not a moment too soon, or I'll go round the bend;
At last, the results — there are lots of surprises —
Good grief! Where's the man who's presenting the prizes?
As you all stream away from the rings and the course,
I'm the only one there who has not seen one horse!

At the end of the day, when you've all had your fun.
There is work for the Secretary still to be done
And, when that is finished, there is next year's event
When I'll be, once again, in the Secretary's tent.

Drawings by John Tickner

Let us Prey

When, up in his pulpit the parson is preaching,
I **know** I should listen to what he is teaching,
But it's not very easy to pray as one ought
When one's thoughts keep on turning to matters of sport.

Forgive me, O Lord, but I know You won't mind,
If I pray that tomorrow in Smith's Gorse we'll find.
May I pray for some guidance on how to shoot straight,
(Would it help if I put a pound coin in the plate?)
May I, as an angler and self-confessed sinner,
Seek Your help in selecting the right fly or spinner.
After climbing for hours and a very long walk,
May I pray for success at the end of a stalk
And, as for that dog which I've raised from a pup,
Please, let him do well in the Waterloo Cup.
Though to have an effect on my spaniel's behaviour
Is, perhaps, asking rather too much of our Saviour,
May I pray for a small slice of Heaven-sent luck
So my hide is in line with the flight of the duck.

Just in case You're becoming a little bit bored
With the prayers of opponents of field sports, Lord,
May I, as a sportsman, for no other reason,
Make a prayer for Your help in the forthcoming season.

Drawings by Carolyn Alexander

Doggerel Days

Aah! He looked so divine when he first became mine —
As a puppy he really was gorgeous —
But, since then, his misdeeds and the lifestyle he leads
Compare badly with those of the Borgias.

Taken out for a walk, he goes off like a cork
From a bottle when let off the lead;
Then we've all got our eyes on the farthest horizon,
Far beyond which he's gone at some speed.

Life has been a bit fraught since the last cat he caught
Was inside him when friends came to call.
"Why, how darling he looks!" he went *books,* books, BOOKS, BOOKS,
And then brought it all up in the hall.

So, to teach the ingredients of some basic obedience,
Off we went to the local dog show,
Where I thought the example of a canine cross-sample
Might teach him some manners — but, no!

It took hours of grooming until he was blooming,
"We will win it," I foolishly told him.
But he blotted his book when he suddenly took
A quick dive and — God knows what he rolled in.

There were dogs thin and fat, dogs resembling a mat,
Dogs of every conceivable height,
Dogs howling, dogs yapping, dogs growling, dogs snapping
And mine — hating each one on sight.

In the tests for agility, his complete inability
Caused each obstacle's disintegration.
When I shouted "Up! Higher!" he leapt into the tyre,
Where he stuck due to overinflation.

Amid shouts of "Disgraceful!" in the race, with his face full
Of dogs' fur, he caused much confusion.
His professional fouls brought crescendoes of howls
And the race to an early conclusion.

My dog's no use at all, he won't come when I call,
He won't "Stay there!" or "Fetch it!" or "Sit!"
All the furniture's gnawed, my commands all ignored,
Except "Heel!" — which he rushed to and bit.

Drawings by John Tickner

A Terrierble Day

Before I took Joe to the Terrier Show
I gave him a much needed bath.
Then, forgetting the need for a collar and lead,
I gave him a walk down the path.

He was off in a flash and at once made a dash
Through the gate and, avoiding recapture,
Proceeded to roll in a very dead mole
With a look on his face of sheer rapture.

Because of the smell, I didn't feel well
In the car. Joe was out in a tick
And started a fight with a dog twice his height
Whose owner joined in with a stick.

This caused a furore and, amidst the uproar,
In less time than it takes in the telling,
The rest had joined in with a terrible din
And their owners all beating and yelling.

At the end of the fight, the ground was a sight,
Bits of debris all over the grass.
A trouser leg here, an ear or two there
When they called: "Can we have the first class?"

Joe just wouldn't budge in front of the judge
Who said, impolitely, "I beg,
Would you please take that thing at once from the ring!"
Joe at once bit him hard on the leg.

The troubles I'd had were not nearly so bad
As the trouble Joe got into next.
He spotted a bitch that he fancied and which
. . . Well, its owner was really quite vexed.

Though Joe can run fast, in his race he was last.
At the start he decided to catch
A large flea in his ear while he sat on his rear,
So he literally started from scratch.

It was no great surprise when I heard that a prize
Had been snatched from the prize-giving table.
So I called it a day and with Joe crept away
Just as quietly as I was able.

I was thankful to go from that Terrier Show
And thus was an awful day ended.
The missing rosette? It was clear who had ate it
When Joe passed a "Highly Commended".

Drawings by John Tickner

ONE OF THE HERD

C.C.

If I were to tell you that, some years ago, and in the space of a fortnight I was mauled by a leopard, shot a crocodile and charged by a rhinoceros, you might think either that I was the devil of a liar or that I could claim some prowess as a white hunter. Neither presumption would be wholly correct, for the bald statements conceal a state of affairs somewhat different to what one might imagine. For a start the leopard was a very small one and happened, at the time, to be under the seat of the car in which I was sitting. The absent-minded owner, with whom I was about to stay, had neglected to give me this vital piece of information and Farouk's sudden objection to my idly dangling hand made me break the world record for the sitting high jump by a margin that would have been even greater had my head not come sharply into contact with the roof while I was still rising at considerable speed.

Moreover, the crocodile was not the monster reptile sometimes encountered in African rivers, but of a size sufficient only to make a handbag and a small pair of shoes when skinned. In my defence I would like to say that being so small, it was all the harder as a target, particularly when standing up in a small boat. Even being charged by a rhino need not necessarily be as frightening as one might imagine. This incident happened when I was stealthily following a tracker on the trail of some water-buck. I had just rounded a large bush which suddenly erupted in the most terrifying snort and a shaking of leaves. The tracker, whose previous experience doubtless alerted him to the fact that we had disturbed the morning sleep of a rhino, disappeared in a grey blur and at a speed that would have won him worldwide acclaim at any Olympic gathering. My reactions were slower. With limbs turned to jelly and feet to lead, I stood rooted to the ground. As it happened, this lack of action was every bit as effective, if not more so, than the instant flight which my brain was quick to order but the aforementioned jellification caused by sheer terror forbade.

The rhino is afflicted with incredibly poor eyesight and when, with a pounding of feet and accelerating fast, this one left his sanctuary, he (or it may have been she since I was hardly in a state to appreciate the finer biological details) failed to notice my presence within five yards. When, some minutes later, the tracker reappeared from the bush wearing a rather shamefaced grin, I was still in precisely the same position and the rhino had gone crashing myopically into the distance. We left the water-buck alone.

This all happened some years ago and my first impression, on returning to East Africa for a fortnight's holiday, was that the herds of people nowadays almost outnumber the animals. Planeloads of Americans, Germans, Dutch, Italians and others disgorge themselves every day on the tarmac at Nairobi. Soon after, they can be observed browsing at numerous waterholes known as 'bars'. Many of the luxury game lodges have a bar conveniently sited so that one's elbow need never be unsupported while watching the denizens of the bush partake of their liquid refreshment.

The most famous of all places from which to watch must be Treetops and, like all good tourists, we paid it a visit. Although the journey up there is accomplished in a Land Rover, the last few hundred yards have to be done on foot, accompanied by a white hunter carrying a large double-barrelled rifle with two bullets at the ready. This seemed a little unnecessary until, shortly after we had gained our objective, a distinctly disgruntled buffalo appeared on the path up which we had so recently walked. The original Treetops was burnt down by the Mau Mau and the new one is on a very grand scale indeed. No less than 70 people can be (and usually are) accommodated every night, a scrumptious tea and sumptuous dinner are served and the cons are extremely mod.

With luck (and we were lucky) some animals arrive at the waterhole in daylight and when photography is still possible. Apart from a number of bush and waterbuck, warthogs and baboons — the latter quickly disposed of a vast cream cake, two scarves, a handbag and one disappeared wearing a rather fetching pullover — the first to arrive was a buffalo. After it had been there for a good twenty minutes, an American lady sitting near me said: "Say, Elmer, have you seen that rhinoceros?" The reply came; "Albie, I do not think that is a rhinoceros, I think that is a bison." The ensuing argument, conducted in a slow mid-Western drawl, continued long after the arrival of some elephants which passed unnoticed by them.

During dinner thirty-five elephants arrived and temporarily disrupted the serving of asparagus, mushroom soup, fillet of beef, sherry trifle and cheese and biscuits. Later they were joined by two more herds, bringing the total at one time up to more than 70, thereby just outnumbering those who were watching them. Not that by any means all the visitors were occupying the various watching points. If the noise of many wild animals — by now, rhinos and buffalo were freely mixing with the elephants — jostling for the salt lick, drinking, performing every kind of ablution and occasionally fighting was considerable, it was no less than that coming from the bar. It seems that, with the coming of darkness, both human beings and animals feel the need for liquid sustenance.

One way to avoid the herds of humans and at the same time to see the wildlife for yourself is to hire a car. Those who are in the car-hire business in Kenya must have worked out that the road surfaces are not conducive to longevity among their charges which are hired out by the mile. Since it is possible, indeed almost essential, to travel huge distances, this can be quite expensive. One is warned never to give a lift since there are, it seems, some fairly unruly characters about. Also the native by the side of the road is, more than likely, only the tip of the iceberg. Hidden from sight but ready to appear at the first sign of a car stopping may be a horde of dependants who will swamp the unsuspecting motorist.

Obadiah was an exception to this rule. He was alone, perfectly respectable and we gave him a lift. Since his destination was only a little way from where we were going and he seemed to have such a high regard for English people, we took him all the way to his home. The decision to do this was one that I found myself regretting as the road deteriorated to a state little better than the surrounding bush. However, we eventually arrived to be introduced to a row of children whose size decreased in direct proportion to their increasing grubbiness until the smallest was little more than a ball of filth. Not entirely to our joy, each one insisted on shaking hands before, with protestations of undying friendship and expressions of hope for our future happy life, Obadiah unwillingly let us go. Had we stayed longer, I have a nasty feeling we would have been introduced to the many animals which doubtless shared his abode, the interior of which we were mercifully spared from seeing.

One goes to East Africa with the certainty of watching a great many animals in their natural state that one would otherwise have only seen, if at all, in a zoo. Equally as fascinating as the ground game are the birds, whether they are in their hundreds of thousands like the flamingo on Lake Nakura or fleetingly seen as they dart away out of sight. During an afternoon spent on Lake Naivasha, it is perfectly easy to record over 100 different species of birds; almost anywhere something as exotic as the long-tailed widow bird or as bright as the superb and glossy starlings can be seen. The only time we played golf, our game was made the more difficult by a ground hornbill which insisted on picking up the balls at every opportunity.

Butterflies, lizards and, along the seashore, wonderful shells, coral and starfish of incredible beauty add to the list of attractions. For anyone in the least interested in wildlife, East Africa is a fascinating place. Where else can one lie in bed and see, on the other side of the Equator, a snow-capped mountain rising majestically from the jungle? Exciting, too, for within the bush lurk elephant, rhino, buffalo, gorillas and many other animals.

The Hunter's Tale

By the fire's dying embers, an old hunter remembers
The days when, more often than not,
Those who didn't endure became lion manure,
Or a stew in a cannibal's pot.

*"Poor old Jim couldn't swim, which was bad luck on him
When a hippo tipped over the boat.
The sound of his cries brought the tears to our eyes
And a lump to a crocodile's throat.*

*Remember O'Grady and that missionary lady
And the natives who made them both martyrs?
Poor miserable sinner, they cooked him for dinner —
While waiting, they had her for starters.*

*Though a bit of a soak, Joe was such a nice bloke
And, in wine, he would frequently say:
'Why are elephants pink?' — but it must have been drink,
He was stepped on by one that was grey.*

*How those bearded, unkempt anthropologists dreamt
Of finding old African cultures.
But the only bones found in small heaps on the ground
Were their own — surrounded by vultures.*

*Billy walked from Mombasa through the swamps to Nyasa,
Watching birds and recording their calls.
So he found it quite easy drifting down the Zambezi
Until (sadly) Victoria Falls.*

*Remember Elfrida? When that buffalo treed her
And she fell, we were close to despair.
But it wasn't too drastic, her knicker elastic
Caught her up and she stopped in mid-air."*

As I sat there enthralled, I was simply appalled
By a rumble which turned me to jelly.
The old man, unperturbed, said: *"Don't be disturbed,
It is only an elephant's belly."*

So, watch out for the snakes, things in rivers and lakes
And keep looking over your shoulder.
There are rhinos and cheetahs, hyenas, man-eaters
And . . . My God! Look what's under that boulder!

Drawings by John Tickner

The Lion's Tale

Grandpapa is a rug in a baronet's snug,
Uncle lies in a duchess's hall,
Poor Mum met her end after eating a friend
Of the Governor — she's on his wall.

Then the bush was all dark, but they've made it a Park
And a place where the tourists can roam;
Just look how they scrimmage while recording my image
To show to the folks back at home.

I'm a very old lion and I'm keeping my eye on
The people all loaded with cameras.
They snap me in flight, while I sleep, when I fight,
Zooming in when I start getting amorous.

I find it frustrating being filmed while I'm mating;
Can you think how an animal feels?
For the old days I sigh as I watch them drive by —
Unobtainable meals on wheels.

Once, a native a day kept our hunger away,
Besides being a tasty comestible,
But now they're all guides driving buses whose hides
I, for one, have found quite indigestible.

Though my ancestors ran at the sound of a man
With his rifle which killed from afar,
Now there's nothing to fear from a gun or a spear —
Just the chance of being hit by a car.

Where very large herds and immense flocks of birds
Used to wander and elephants lumbered,
Now those columns of dust come from tourists embussed
To see animals they have outnumbered.

The buffalo, rhino and most leopards I know,
Who once were considered big game,
And the cheetah, the bongo and crocs in the Congo
Are, I fear, getting terribly tame.

The spirit has died in my family pride,
Life's become an intolerable bore.
As the tourist trade grows I do nothing but pose —
I can hardly be bothered to roar.

Drawings by John Tickner

The Encyclopedia of Animal Life . . .

The AARD-VARK is an ant-bear,
An eater-up of ants.
He has to vark extremely aard
To get just vat he vants.

The BISON is not beautiful
Nor the desert that he stands in.
The Bison also is a thing
Australians wash their hands in.

In Africa, the River Nile
Is haunted by the CROCODILE,
Whose habits, smell and toothy smile
Make me, for one, no crocophile.
Natives being two a penny,
That crocodiles consumed so many
Was not thought unduly cruel
Under old colonial rule.
Then things changed and what they ate
Became a matter for the State.
The contents of a croc's inside
Are swallowed now with national pride.

... From A to E

DUNG-BEETLE, what a curious name!
But stranger still his favourite game,
Daily pushing fro and to
An evil smelling lump of goo,
Until, one day, he meets his bride
Who, blushing, pops an egg inside.
It lies there steaming in the sun —
It's like an oven in the bun.
Then from within that stinking turd
The sound of tiny feet is heard.
Three tiny pairs of feet appear,
Excitement grows, "Why, look, my dear!"
Ah, then what cries of beetle joy —
"My darling, it's a beetle boy!"

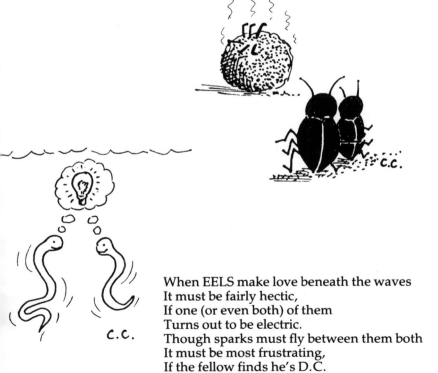

When EELS make love beneath the waves
It must be fairly hectic,
If one (or even both) of them
Turns out to be electric.
Though sparks must fly between them both
It must be most frustrating,
If the fellow finds he's D.C.
And his girl friend alternating.

Pony Tales

Trials and Tribulations

We've driven for miles to the pony club trials
With their usual ghastly frustrations
And, as likely as not, it will all be for what?
Just two more e-liminations.

When our daughter went first, we both feared the worst —
And how justified were all our fears —
For, just as I reckoned, she stopped at the second
And promptly dissolved into tears.

She baulked at the third and used a rude word,
Which was new to the judge (so he said),
And then at the fourth, when the pony took off,
She fell in the ditch on her head.

She got on again and grinned through the pain,
As she flew over five, six and seven,
But, turning too late, she never saw eight
And galloped straight on to eleven.

All over the ground the ponies rush round
Under children of varying abilities.
And the standard of food? — Well it's, frankly, not good —
On a par with the toilet facilities.

"Get on with it, child!" shouts a father, quite wild,
And a mother comes galloping through.
As they run the course, their voices all hoarse,
You would think they had entered it too.

"Now son, are you ready? Then just take it steady,
You're next to go after the grey."
Oh! I say, what hard luck! Just a kick and a buck
And he's off, but in quite the wrong way.

He's quick to remount and the fall doesn't count,
He's away — and the family cheers.
But, alas, at the double he got into trouble
And the only hope now is the pairs.

When they set off again it had started to rain
And they came back all covered in mud.
They'd got caught together and broken a leather
And a fetlock was streaming with blood.

When you think of the sweat (and we're not back home yet)
And the tears and the rage and the sorrow.
Though it's meant to be fun, I, for one, am quite done
And, my God! There's another tomorrow!

Drawings by John Tickner

Thereby Hangs a Tail

When the summer term ended last week,
For us ponies the outlook is bleak.
We inwardly groan as
Our jodhpured young owners
Descend on our field with a shriek.

Our bellies blown out like balloons,
Every morning and most afternoons
We're sure to be spending
In jumping and bending
Or trying to keep eggs in their spoons.

At gymkhanas we're in for a drubbing
As our riders, all kicking and scrubbing,
Either leap off our backs
And jump into sacks
Or fall by mistake and start blubbing.

The children all love fancy dress,
Though each year we enjoy it much less
As White Knight and Charger,
As Jumbo and Rajah,
Wells Fargo and Pony Express.

As for charity, think of us while
Riders, sponsored, just sit there in style
Simply cutting a dash
As they rake in the cash
— for MILE after MILE after MILE.

At eventing cross-countries we do
Quite well, in the show jumping too.
But, as for the dressage,
We don't get the message
And the penalties? Three sixty-two!

Then that week which we all spend together
At Pony Club camp and the weather
Brings millions of flies,
So it's no great surprise
When we come to the end of our tether.

In mid-August we're starting to droop
When, at rallies, we're put in a group.
In singles and pairs,
In circles and squares
We are drilled like a cavalry troop.

By September we're just about done,
But the children are still having fun,
Putting cups onto poles
And potatoes in bowls
And, perhaps, a rosette to be won.

Then the nights seem incredibly short
And we don't always do what we ought.
Preferring our grass
To a Pony Club class,
We simply refuse to be caught.

No, it's not very hard to remember
Those weeks from July to September.
You can understand why
We will all heave a sigh
When they go back to school till December.

Drawings by John Tickner

HANDS UP!

" Good box . . .

. . . shoe . . .

The progressive enlargement of little girls is, as the late Maurice Chevalier put it so neatly in song and a charming French accent, a matter of every day fact. The same applies to little boys. Little ponies, however, remain exactly the same size.

It follows, therefore that the initial purchase of a small pony will lead inexorably to further acquisitions with a greater load-bearing capability and it is worth mentioning that the intervals between buying one and needing another are extremely short. The size of ponies being gauged in hands, it is also perhaps noteworthy that the rising scale in hand measurement is matched by the increasing depth to which one's own hand must be dipped into the economic pocket.

There is a certain awful inevitability about the whole process, a process, I might add, that starts so innocently and without warning of what is to follow, that many a normally intelligent parent has taken the first irrevocable step quite unaware of where the path is leading. It is like watching a non-swimmer, heedless of one's shouted warning, walking out towards a ledge hidden beneath the water.

Aha! You may say. This is not for me. But I am prepared

138

to lay odds that, if you are already a parent or thinking of becoming one and have access to a few square yards of grass, you will one day find yourself the proud possessor of a small hairy quadruped at the flanks of which your first-born's heels will be busily scrubbing in an effort to achieve some forward movement.

I know — I've been there. It seems only yesterday, though it certainly was not, that my daughter could be seen, one arm affectionately around a diminutive Blackie's neck, the other stuffing peppermints into the pony's mouth. Later, huge animals bore menacingly down on me when I approached their field, demanding an ever larger share of oats, bran and other expensive fuels.

Since this is a cautionary note, let me start by saying that the process can start in any one of a number of different ways. Maybe it is: "Daddy, the Joneses are moving and wondered if we would like to have their donkey." Or, "Daddy, I went riding on Mandy's pony and it was such fun. Could I have a pony. Please, Daddy, please." Any hesitation on the doting parental part at this point is fatal.

Assuming that the fatal hesitation did occur, the next step is to buy a pony. One method is to peruse the advertisement columns of some suitable periodical and this will open up to you a whole new world of fascinating reading, the advertisers having paid the maximum regard to the cost per word and the minimum concessions to English grammar. Take, for example, "Good box, shoe, clip. Safe traffic. Excellent jump, great character, £350 ono." Oh, no, indeed! As far as I am concerned, great characters are for other people and that excellent jump may refer to the boundary fence. And no mention of catching — watch it.

Having made one's selection from columns full of similarly cryptic descriptions, the next step is to go and have a look. The prospective purchase is probably tied up and neatly groomed, but be sure to notice if there are any red faces among the welcoming party — a possible sign that they have spent the last two hours trying to round the wretched animal up. Frayed ropes and chafed hands, news that the local blacksmith is in hospital and sprouts of uncut hair in various places may well indicate that "Good box, shoe, clip," did not tell the whole story.

While, on the one hand, it is sensible to ask for a practical demonstration of behaviour in traffic, it is not normally necessary to forearm oneself with a hand grenade to test the advertisement's claim of 'Bombproof' at first hand. A modicum of descriptive licence must be allowed for.

Having arrived at the point where an offer is about to be made for a pony and subject to such formalities as a veterinary inspection, gamesmanship comes into play. Should you have been so injudicious as to turn up in a brand new car and with the tan of an expensive foreign holiday still plainly visible on your face, the seller will know that his asking price is well within your capability. Furthermore, he will have noted any over-enthusiastic reaction on the part of your offspring, which may make it well nigh impossible for you to break off proceedings.

On his part, the seller will have doubtless carefully briefed his own child or kept it out of sight, in case an indiscreet remark might upset the applecart. Nothing is calculated quicker to bring to an end a potentially profitable transaction than the exposure of a part of an anatomy and "Look where Bonny bit me," or "I couldn't go to the gymkhana yesterday as I couldn't catch the pony."

There are, of course, sources other than advertisements via which you may acquire a pony. Friends, for instance. The danger here is that, by the time you have graduated from leading rein, through gymkhanas and hunter trials, to the higher echelons of equestrian eventing, you will have lost a lot of friends. The chances are, within an hour or so of concluding a deal with a friend, you will have heard of another pony half the price and twice as suitable. Or, worse, meeting another friend you will be told, "Surely you knew that pony has . . ." And here will follow, if you are lucky, something mild like the quaintly described ". . . a stop in it," or, if you are less fortunate, a lurid description of some ghastly disease which only becomes apparent the following summer.

By the way, you have included the cost of a trailer in your calculations? And the fitting of a towbar — to the possibly larger car you will need? Then there is that conglomeration of leather and metal referred to as tack, suitable clothing, fodder, the availability of a blacksmith — ah, but the list is endless.

But don't, please, let me put you off. If the prospect of a friendless life, punctuated by frequent visits to the bank manager, does not daunt you — by all means carry on. Remember, though, you have not yet reached the first fence. When you do, it may well be that you find yourself faced with the tearful consequences of the first of many refusals.

. . . clip."

They're Back!

As I lean on the gate, I say, "Ponies just wait!
Make the most of that grass while you can.
From now on each day it's a netful of hay
And a handful of nuts and some bran.

"Yes, those darlings are back and they're cleaning their tack,
So just you take heed of my warning.
They're back for the holidays, Christmas and jolly days
And we're off to the meet in the morning!"

"Mummy! Somebody's sat on the brim of my hat."
"Where's my hairnet?" the other one yells.
And then there's a panic when something organic
Is found in a boot — and it smells.

With a popping of stitches they squeeze in their breeches
And boots which are sizes too small,
Then a pony gets free. It's a wonder to me
That they ever get hunting at all.

At the meet there's a dash and gone in a flash
Are the trayfuls of food and the port.
And there's one little lad (he takes after dad)
Who drinks a lot more than he ought.

Says the General to me, "Got the brats out I see,
There'll be trouble today to be sure."
At once he's proved right when, his horse, taking fright,
Bucks him off in a heap of manure.

At the very first fence, rushing hither and thence,
The ponies go faster and faster.
With pigtails a-flying, two girls fall off crying
While a third gallops under the Master.

With his face turning black, the Master rides back.
Shouts a squeaky voice, "Make way for Sir!"
But a Shetland defeats him and promptly unseats him,
Its leading rein caught round his spur.

By a quarter to two there are only a few
Still attempting to follow the horn.
The rest have got cold, fallen off or been told
To go home in a rage — and they've gorn.

Her tummy is aching, so Mummy is taking
The younger one back in the box.
But somewhere or other, I fear that her brother
Is still in pursuit of the fox.

I seek him in vain over hill, farm and lane
Till it's dark and my temper is thin.
But then with a rush he comes up with the brush
And from one ear to t'other a grin.

With the hols just begun and with miles yet to run
In pursuit on my feet like a fool,
It isn't the **sheep** that I count going to sleep
But the **days** till they go back to school.

Illustrated by John Tickner

Hands Up! (again)

Every year, as children grow,
New ponies come, old ponies go.
An ancient moke began the chain
And next we bought a leading rein.
Then, hand by hand, right up the scale
We followed on the pony trail.

Each new arrival's met with cheers
And each departure, floods of tears,
As frantic mums and dads as well
All beg and borrow, buy and sell.
The lines are humming with the news
Of shetlands, arabs, 14.2's.

"Oh darling, tell me what to do,
I'm DES-perate for a 13.2
Now Paul has grown far too tall
For Merrilegs and Jane's too small.
That arab mare of Mary Brown?
My dear, it's TWELVE and broken down."

"Did you hear what happened while
The Smiths had Merrilegs on trial?
They SAY he bolted, now he's lame
And, frankly dear, he's not the same.
That grey you said that we should see
Was full of worms and 13.3."

"We're in the market once again,
We need another one for Jane.
I think that roan has got a stop
And is it WISE to do a swop?
Can you tell me what its height is?
Is it prone to laminitis?"

"I don't know WHAT to do with Paul.
He hardly ever rides at all.
And, after you know what, I fear
Poor Jane can't go to camp this year.
That dun we bought won't jump, alas,
Old Merrilegs is out to grass."

And now the sands of time have run,
With ponies we have nearly done.
The years of shows and rallies past,
Rosettes on walls are fading fast.
So, do you know of someone who
Might like to buy a 15.2?

Drawings by John Tickner

Beakies

The Beakies

A Beakie is a person
Resembling a bird,
Whose habits and appearance
Are patently absurd.
I wonder if you've met one,
For I've met quite a few;
And, if you haven't met one,
Are you sure one isn't you?

THE POTBELLIED PUFFIN
(weesi rotunda)

The Potbellied Puffin is a large ungainly bird incapable of high-speed flight. Its plumage is often richly checkered.

Voice: When trying to gain height, a wheezing sound. During frequent pauses it utters a plaintive *hangonaminit* or *isaysteddionthairoldboi*.

Habitat: Normally an urban resident, but can be seen on the moors (August), cornstubbles (September) and in woodlands (November-January).

THE INFAMOUS GROUSE
(dramo drambui)

The Infamous Grouse is a bird of rich and widely varied plumage, noted for its uncertain temper (particularly the morning after) and its unwillingness to share its favourite food with others.

Voice: An occasional *hootsmon* or *ocheye*. Also *eylltakadramwi'ee*. Sometimes makes a piping sound.

Habitat: Originating from Scotland, where its nesting sites are known as distilleries, it is now seen all over the world.

THE REDBREASTED HORNBLOWER
(tallio tallio)

The Redbreasted Hornblower is easily recognised by its bright scarlet plumage and black, rounded top of head.

Voice: A merry trumpeting emitted when in pursuit of its quarry. When aroused, it is capable of an amazing variety of calls, an example of which is *oldaardywbluddiphools*.

Habitat: Seen mostly in winter, widespread in Britain with the exception of northern Scotland. Often appears in company with huge flocks of Thrusters, Brown-breasted Bowlers, Hedge Larks, Hedge Cuckoos (or Stopcocks) and Flatcapped Petrols.

THE TANGLED KNOT
(piscator frustratus)

The Tangled Knot is a green legged wader and a rather ineffective predator of fish. Similar to the Fluent Caster, but with more jerky movements and closely related to the Common Thrash.

Voice: When standing with wings outstretched *yewshoodavseenthewunthatgottaway*.

Habitat: Widespread in and around most rivers, canals and lakes. More active than the Green-Brollied Dipper which shares its habitat.

THE STONED CURLEW
(blotto frequentia)

The Stoned Curlew can be identified by its erratic flight
and bemused expression. Often falls off its perch. Many
birds can be recognised by a distinctive bar on the wings;
the Stoned Curlew, however, often has its wing on a bar.

Voice: A loud and often repeated *maykitalarjwunskwyre*
and *shaymagane* with an occasional *hic*.

Habitat: A local resident, spending much time in The
Elms, The Old Oak Tree, The Yew Tree and others,
sometimes in company with The Golden Pheasant, Black
Swan, Ruddy Duck, White Hart and, surprisingly, Fox
and Hounds.

THE HOORAY HOOPOE
(chinlis wunda)

The Hooray Hoopoe is often seen in large parties, throwing its food around indiscriminately. Very noisy and upwardly mobile.

Voice: A rather drawly *oheyesaychairpslettsavsumbubbli*.

Habitat: Tends to congregate in the region of Sloane Square, London. Regular migratory routes include those to Ascot, Henley, Goodwood, Badminton, etc.

C.C.

THE GLOSSY-CRESTED THRUSTER
(Celer maximus)

The Glossy-Crested Thruster: This superb looking bird can be identified by its tall black glossy crest and tremendous speed of flight, going long distances in a straight line. The bird illustrated is the Old English or Edwardian Thruster which is now rare and can be distinguished from other varieties by the swallow-tail. Both males and females have spurs, but only males have the tall crest.

Voice: A loud chattering when gathered in flocks, but mostly silent when in flight apart from the occasional *gerroutomiway*.

Habitat: Same as for the Hornblower with which it frequently associates. The Thruster sometimes flies so fast that it outstrips the Hornblower — never more than once in a day though. When first seen in early autumn the Thruster is in moult, drab in colour and virtually flightless, almost indistinguishable from the Ratcatcher or Brown-Breasted Bowler. It regains its full glorious plumage and flight feathers early in November.

152

C.C.

THE SECRETARY BIRD
(capu capu)

The Secretary Bird: A sharp pair of eyes are needed to spot the Secretary Bird (or Capper, as it is sometimes known). With its round, black-topped head, and a red or black body, it hides among similarly plumaged birds while stalking its prey. Even the wariest of birds have been known to be fooled by its ability to go into sudden moult and then pounce from behind a hedge. Thus it often catches the nimble Stint.

Voice: Although a quiet bird, its voice has become noticeably more strident in recent years. Whereas, a short time ago it used to call *tenbobplees*, more urgent cries of *itsatenna* and even a repeated *twenti* and *twentifyv* have recently been recorded. Sometimes known to make a chinking sound while in flight.

Habitat: Its most frequently noted perch is near open gateways. A solitary bird, but usually moves around among Thrusters, Ratcatchers etc. Resident birds normally escape its attentions, but migratory birds, particularly the late arrivals, often fall prey to the Capper.

C.C.

THE TWEEDIE DAPPER
(frequentia syndicatus)

The Tweedie Dapper: The British native Dapper (seen here on its usual perch) is rather drab in appearance, though foreign visitors of the same species tend to be much more gaudy in their plumage. The Tweedie Dapper can easily be recognised by its habit of gathering in small flocks of eight or ten, then separating and sitting motionless for long periods about 30 yards apart.

Voice: A rather drawn out *ovah* (not to be confused with the Common Ruff's more abrupt *ova*). In January the Dapper's call tends to change slightly to *cokovah*.

Habitat: First sightings usually occur on or around August 12 on moorlands in Scotland and the north of England. In September the Dapper migrates to lower ground, mostly open farmland, before moving into woodlands during the winter months. Last sightings are towards the end of January, after which the Dapper disappears from the country scene.

154

C.C.

THE GREEN-BROLLIED DIPPER
(piscator somnambulus)

The Green-Brollied Dipper: Being the only bird in the world to build its nest upside down (as shown above), the Green-Brollied Dipper can easily be recognised. Furthermore, having built this strange nest, it then sits motionless under the nest for hours on end, apparently hoping to lull its prey into a false sense of security.

Voice: A continuous snoring sound..

Habitat: Most commonly seen on the banks of canals and rivers. Huge flocks foregather at weekends and then spread out along the river banks, each bird building its own nest only a yard or two from the next. Having built the nest, the Dipper then remains in it for the rest of the day at the end of which it retires to its roost, which is usually in a nearby town.

Tailpiece

IN CONCLUSION, or, if you have opened this book at the back, as an INTRODUCTION, I would like to pay tribute to Dr. Wuntz, the well-known ornithologist, who gave his name to the bird he discovered. He has kindly allowed me to reproduce here the only picture ever taken of the bird which, so far as is known, has never been seen again.

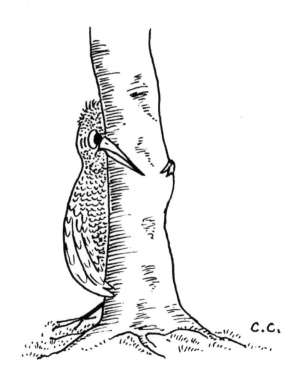

WUNTZ BITTERN — a very shy bird